Counsel
to
Counsel

Counsel
to
Counsel

From Practice to Business:
Build the Law Firm That Works for You

Emil Abedian, CPA

MUNN
AVENUE
PRESS

COUNSEL TO COUNSEL
From Practice to Business:
Build the Law Firm That Works for You

Published by
Munn Avenue Press
300 Main Street, Ste 21
Madison, NJ 07940
MunnAvenuePress.com

A MUNN AVENUE PRESS

Paperback ISBN: 978-1-960299-77-2
Hardcover ISBN: 978-1-960299-78-9

Printed in the United States of America

Contents

Introduction

I was four years old when my world changed forever. In that year of 1984, my family had just fled Iran in the wake of the Iranian revolution and in the middle of the Gulf War. We were Armenian Christians—immigrants for generations in Iran, descendants of skilled craftsmen brought over centuries ago by Persian kings. But now, like so many others caught in the upheaval, we found ourselves starting over in a new land: Sweden.

One of my earliest memories of that time is standing in my aunt's apartment in Uppsala, the unfamiliar scent of cardamom coffee hanging in the air. After six months without him, I couldn't stop staring at my father—his familiar smile, the way his eyes crinkled at the corners, the strong hands I remembered holding mine. The apartment was crowded with relatives, their voices a mix of Armenian and Swedish, but I stayed glued to Dad's side, clutching his hand as if he might disappear again.

"Well," my mother said with a tired smile, ruffling my hair, "now you've seen your father. Time to head back home."

The words hit me like a splash of cold water. Hot tears welled up instantly, and I wrapped both arms around my father's leg, pressing my face against his knee. "No, no, no!" The thought of losing him again was unbearable.

The room went silent. My mother's face fell as she realized her mistake, and she quickly knelt beside me. "Emil, mama jan (sweetheart in Armenian), I was only joking. We're staying here, all of us together." She pulled me into her arms, murmuring soft words in Armenian while my father's hand came to rest on my shoulder. Even at four, I understood in that moment that "home" had shifted—it wasn't a place anymore, but wherever we could be together.

But here's the thing about starting over: it forces you to see the world differently. While most Swedish kids were being ferried to soccer practice by their parents, I and my immigrant friends were taking the bus or riding our bikes. My father worked seven days a week at his Persian restaurant, and my mother juggled a job at a preschool with raising three kids. We were definitely not wealthy, but we had enough—enough for me to join the soccer team, enough to dream bigger dreams.

That immigrant drive never left me. Even after graduating from university and landing a position at Ernst & Young in Stockholm, I felt the pull to prove myself, to do more, to be better. It's what eventually brought me to Los Angeles in 2007, where a summer vacation turned into meeting my future wife, Narineh. Together, we now have two wonderful sons, William, 12, and Henry, 8. What was supposed to be a one-year experiment became the foundation of my life's work.

Today, I run one of the most specialized CPA firms in America, focused exclusively on helping law firms transform their practices into thriving businesses. The lessons I learned as that little boy in Sweden—about adaptation, about seeing opportunities where others see obstacles, about the power of systems and support networks—have shaped every aspect of how I approach business transformation.

This book isn't just about accounting or law firm management. It's about seeing your practice through fresh eyes, the way an immigrant must see their new world. It's about understanding that being an excellent attorney isn't enough; you need to be an excellent business owner too. And most importantly, it's about escaping the trap that so many talented lawyers fall into: working harder instead of smarter, wearing too many hats, and watching their dreams of independence turn into a hamster wheel of endless tasks.

I meet lawyers every day who tell me the same story: "Emil, I'm drowning. I'm working more hours than ever, but billing less. I'm constantly overwhelmed, trying to be everything to everyone." Sound familiar? Just last month, a highly successful IP attorney came to me six months after starting his own practice. He had the clients, he had the expertise, but he was spending more time on administrative tasks than actual legal work. His story—which we'll explore in detail later—is just one example of the challenges this book will help you overcome.

What you'll find in these pages is a blueprint for transformation, one that I've refined over years of working exclusively with law firms. We'll cover everything from operational efficiency to profit maximization, from team building to client attraction. But more than that, we'll explore how to shift your mindset from being just a lawyer to being a business owner who happens to practice law.

This isn't theory. Every strategy, every system, every piece of advice in this book has been battle-tested in real law firms, with real attorneys facing the same challenges you're facing right now. I've lived these same challenges myself, building and growing my CPA firm over the past 15 years. The parallels between running a law practice and an accounting firm are striking; we face the same operational hurdles, growth challenges, and administrative headaches. The lessons I've learned, often the hard way, translate directly to law firm management. Whether you're a solo practitioner drowning in administrative tasks or a small firm looking to scale, you'll find practical, actionable solutions to your most pressing problems—solutions proven effective not just in my clients' law firms, but in my own professional practice as well.

So, are you ready to transform your practice? Let's begin.

CHAPTER 1

Chasing Your Tail

I once worked with a hotshot lawyer—let's call her Ms. IP (for Intellectual Property)—who decided she had had enough of sharing the spoils with her partners. She had been killing it at her firm, so why not go solo and keep all that delicious profit for herself? Sounds like the dream, right?

Fast forward six months and our heroine is drowning in her own success. Clients? She's got 'em. Money? It's flowing in. But she's working harder than ever and taking home less than she did at the firm. Talk about a plot twist!

See, Ms. IP thought she was just buying her freedom. Instead, she bought herself a one-way ticket to Overwhelm City, population: her. By day, she was juggling client work, marketing, and admin tasks like a circus performer on steroids. By night, she was burning the midnight oil, drowning in a sea of invoices and collection calls.

The cherry on top of this chaos sundae? She was so busy playing marketer, IT director, HR manager, and bookkeeper that she was turning away clients. That's right, money was literally walking out the door because our legal eagle couldn't find the time to spread her wings.

• •

But here's where it gets really juicy. Ms. IP was caught in a classic catch-22. She needed to keep marketing to fill her pipeline for the next few months, but she was so swamped with current work that she could barely breathe, let alone network. And don't even get me started on the collection calls. Nothing says "thanks for your business" like hounding a client for payment.

The irony was that Ms. IP left the bigger firm to make more money and have a more flexible schedule that worked for her and her family, but she had become a slave to her own ambition. She was trapped on a hamster wheel of her own making, running faster and faster but getting nowhere. Instead of building a sustainable business, she'd essentially bought herself a very demanding job—one that paid well but required her constant presence. Without her, everything would grind to a halt. She hadn't created a firm, she'd created a high-paying prison with herself as both warden and inmate.

This is what I often call "buying yourself employment" rather than building a business. Yes, you might make good money, but if your firm can't function without you physically being there, you don't own a business. The business owns you. True entrepreneurship means building something that can thrive even when you step away. Now here is another example from the other end of the spectrum. One time, I went to visit an old client of mine who was just opening a new firm in downtown Los Angeles, back when it was still buzzing with life, not the ghost town it became post-COVID. I was walking into a high-rise that screamed "success" from every polished surface. The elevator dinged, the doors slid open, and I stepped into what looked like a law firm on steroids.

Allen and his new partner greeted me. They were standing in 4,000+ square feet of prime real estate, surrounded by enough empty desks to seat a small army. But guess what? It was just the two of them, grinning like cats who got the cream.

Now, most people would think these guys had lost their marbles. But let me tell you, this wasn't madness, this was method.

These guys had a vision, and they weren't afraid to fake it till they made it. They knew that in the world of law, perception is reality. They looked big, they thought big, they acted big, and guess what? They became big.

Fast forward to today, and these two ambitious attorneys have gone from empty desks to a staff of 150. They've traded their rented space for their own building near the Crypto Arena (formerly Staples Center). One of them is even a regular on news channels, a bona fide celebrity attorney.

As Neama (the celebrity partner) told me, "There's no freaking way we could handle 150 employees ourselves. We put the right people in place; they oversee what needs to be done and they report to us. We set the plans, and they execute. If we don't see the results we want, that's when they have to justify why. Otherwise, we're golden."

This, my friends, is how you go from zero to hero in the legal world. In less than a decade, these guys went from two men in an oversized office to a 150-strong legal powerhouse.

The Dream vs. The Reality

The life of a solo practitioner or small firm lawyer is often romanticized as the pinnacle of legal entrepreneurship. But the hard data paints a sobering picture of the challenges these professionals face daily.

Let's start with the brutal truth about billable hours. On average, lawyers are only spending 2.9 hours per day on billable work.[1] That's a mere 37% of a standard workday. They bill 2.6 hours and collect only 2.3 hours. For small firm owners, this isn't just a statistic, it's a financial guillotine hanging over their heads. Every non-billable hour is potential revenue slipping through their fingers. But here's the kicker: it's not that they're lazy. Far from it. They're drowning in administrative tasks, client hand-holding, and the endless juggling act of running a business.

Now, let's talk about money left on the table. Lawyers are billing less than 90% of their billable work and collecting a mere 88% of what they bill.[2] Do the math, and you'll see that the average lawyer is earning only about 29% of their theoretical yearly billing amount. For a solo or small firm, that's not

---

[1] 2024 Clio Legal Trend Report.

[2] Ibid.

just lost profit, it's the difference between thriving and barely surviving.

But why is this happening? It's a perfect storm of inefficiency and overwhelm. Small firm lawyers are often so busy putting out fires that they can't focus on the activities that actually generate revenue. They're stuck in a vicious cycle: too busy to bill properly, too overwhelmed to chase payments, and too stressed to strategize for growth.

Adding fuel to this fire is the modern client's expectations. A whopping 79% of consumers expect lawyers to be responsive outside of business hours. For the solo practitioner, this means being perpetually on call, blurring the lines between work and personal life. It's a recipe for burnout that makes sustainable growth feel like an impossible dream.

Technology could be the lifeline these lawyers need. Firms using multiple technologies saw 40% more revenue growth. But here's the rub: adopting new tech requires time and mental bandwidth, two resources in critically short supply for overwhelmed small firm owners. They're stuck in a Catch-22, too busy to implement the very solutions that could free up their time.

Even simple changes, like offering credit card payments (preferred by 82% of clients while many solo and small firms report that they do not offer these payment options), feel like monumental tasks when you're barely keeping your head above water. Every change, no matter how beneficial in the long run, feels like another item on an already impossible to-do list.

The result? A profession full of talented, hardworking individuals who are stuck in survival mode. They can't grow because they're too busy staying afloat. They can't delegate because they can't afford to hire. They can't streamline because they don't have time to step back and strategize.

This is the critical juncture where many small firms get stuck. The owners are working harder than ever, but progress feels impossible. The overwhelm isn't just a phase; it becomes the defining feature of their professional lives. Breaking free from this cycle isn't just about working harder; it requires a fundamental shift in how these lawyers approach their practice and their business.

Let's talk about why most lawyers come knocking on our door. It's not because they're swimming in their spare time or because they love switching accountants. No, it's because they're stuck in financial quicksand, and their current CPA is throwing them a rope made of wet spaghetti.

Here's the deal: Most lawyers are working with CPAs who are about as proactive as a sloth on vacation. These accountants show up once a year, like some kind of tax season Santa Claus, fiddle with some half-baked numbers from a bookkeeper, file a return, and then vanish into the night. Great if you're running a lemonade stand. Not so great if you're trying to build a legal empire.

Let's explore a few of the areas that tend to trip up most solo practitioners or small firms into a quagmire of quicksand:

Time: The Silent Killer of Solo Practices

You've passed the bar, cut your teeth at a big firm, and now you're ready to hang your own shingle. Congratulations, counselor, you're about to embark on the rollercoaster ride of running your own law practice. Buckle up, because it's going to be one hell of a trip.

Let's start with the cold, hard truth: Time is about to become your worst enemy and your most precious commodity. It's the biggest problem I see with any professional trying to run their own firm, but for lawyers? It's like trying to catch smoke with your bare hands.

Here's the typical scene: You've spent years making someone else rich. You've billed more hours than there are stars in the sky, and you've finally had enough. *I can do this for myself,* you think. And you know what? You're absolutely right. You can do this for yourself. But you're about to find out that doing it for yourself means doing everything yourself.

The Honeymoon Phase

At first, it's exhilarating. You're designing business cards that don't have someone else's name above yours. You're creating a website that reflects your vision, not some stuffy partner's idea of what a law firm should look like. You're the captain now, and the ship is yours to steer.

But here's what they don't tell you in law school: Running a law firm is nothing like practicing law. Suddenly, you're not just an attorney. You're a marketer, an accountant, an IT specialist, a human resources department, and oh yeah, you still need to practice law somewhere in between all of that.

This is usually when the panic sets in. This is when lawyers reach out to us, eyes wide with the realization that they're in way over their heads. And you know what? That's okay. That's smart, actually. Because recognizing you need help is the first step to creating a law firm that works for you, instead of the other way around.

The Investment Mindset

Now, let's talk about a mindset shift that can change everything: the difference between an expense and an investment.

Most lawyers fresh out on their own see everything as an expense. New software? Expense. Marketing budget? Expense. Hiring help? Big expense. But here's the truth. If you're only looking at expenses, you're playing not to lose instead of playing to win.

Let's break it down with a couple of examples:

Buying a fancy car for your firm? That's an expense. Sure, it might make you feel good pulling up to the courthouse, but it's not bringing in new clients or making your practice more efficient.

On the flip side, subscribing to a practice management software, attending a business trade show or hiring team members? That's an investment. It helps you run your firm more efficiently so you can put your time in the right place, where it really matters. It's the gift that keeps on giving.

The Financial Crystal Ball

But how do you know if you can afford to make these investments? This is where most solo practitioners and small firms drop the ball. They're flying blind, financially speaking.

If you don't have accurate, up-to-date financial information, you're making decisions based on gut feelings and whatever happens to be in your bank account at the moment. That's like trying to navigate a ship by guessing which way the wind is blowing.

You might look at your bank balance, see $50,000, and think you're flush with cash. But without a clear financial picture, you don't know about the $40,000 in bills coming due next week or the fact that you haven't paid yourself in two months.

This financial fog leads to one of two equally disastrous scenarios:

1. You're too cautious, missing out on opportunities to grow your practice because you're afraid to spend money.

2. You're too optimistic, spending money you don't really have and digging yourself into a hole.

Neither of these is a recipe for success. What you need is clarity. You need systems that give you a real-time view of your financial health, so you can make informed decisions about where to invest in your practice.

The Path Forward

So, what's the solution to this time crunch and financial blindness? It's not about working harder; I guarantee you're already working harder than you ever did at your old firm. It's about working smarter.

It's about setting up systems that automate the parts of your practice that don't require your legal expertise. It's about getting the right help—not just warm bodies to fill seats, but strategic partners who can take entire chunks of work off your plate.

And most importantly, it's about having the financial clarity to make smart decisions about your practice. Because here's the truth: Every hour you spend on admin work, on trying to figure out your finances, on anything that isn't practicing law or strategically growing your firm, is an hour you're leaving money on the table.

In the next chapter, we're going to dive into exactly how to set up these systems, how to get the help you need, and how to gain the financial clarity that will let you make power moves in your practice. Because you didn't go solo to become a slave to your firm. You went solo to build something amazing. And with the right approach, that's exactly what you're going to do. But first, here is a little success story just so you won't think I'm all about the *sturm* and *drang* (storm and stress, to borrow from an old German saying!).

Eddie's Story

Eddie is a young lawyer who was flying blind before he found us. Eddie was stuck in the dark ages, financially speaking. He'd get his tax return and it might as well have been written in hieroglyphics. His bookkeeper's numbers and his CPA's figures were playing a game of mismatched socks, and his CPA's explanation? "Trust me, this is good for you." Spoiler alert: It wasn't.

Eddie was trying to run a growing law firm without knowing his numbers. It's like trying to fly a plane with a blindfold on—exciting, sure, but not exactly a recipe for success. He couldn't make decisions about hiring, expanding, or investing because he was playing financial Russian roulette every day.

But here's where it gets good. Someone introduced Eddie to us, and suddenly, it was like someone turned on the lights at a really depressing party. We didn't just crunch his numbers, we made those numbers sing and dance for him. Regular meetings, real-time updates, actual strategic planning—you know, the stuff that helps you build a business instead of just running on a hamster wheel.

Four years later, Eddie's firm has quadrupled in size. He's gone from five employees to over 20. And the best part? He knows exactly where he stands financially at any given moment. He's not just working in his business, he's working on his business.

See, that's the difference between an expense and an investment. An expense is buying a Ferrari to impress clients (newsflash: no one's hiring you because of your car). An investment is having financial clarity that lets you make bold moves, like having the courage to put the right people in the right seats.

The point is that you can't make smart decisions with dumb data. You need real-time, accurate financial information to fuel your growth. Otherwise, you're just another lawyer hoping your bank account has enough cushion to soften the blow of your next credit card bill.

One of my clients' stories really illustrates the common struggles I see with small firms. Zach (not his real name) came to me about seven years ago with what seemed like a paradox. He was drowning in work but not making enough money.

Zach had done what most successful attorneys do. He'd established a solid reputation, built a client base, and even started hiring a small team. He'd invested in top-tier practice management software (Clio), thinking technology would solve his problems. But here was the catch: He was so busy trying to keep up with client work that he never had time to implement the software or properly train his team.

When I drove down to his Newport Beach office for our first meeting, I found a classic case of what I call "success drowning." His team wanted to help but lacked clear direction. His software sat largely unused. And most tellingly, his billing was months behind.

We started with the fundamentals—getting his billing

process working smoothly, not by doing the legal work, but by implementing systems that ensured invoices went out promptly after services were provided. This made an immediate difference. When clients receive bills while they still clearly remember the value you delivered, they're much less likely to question the charges or delay payment.

The transformation was remarkable. Clients stopped calling to negotiate discounts. Payments came in faster. And, by implementing electronic payment options through email and text message links, we cut collection time in half. That's not just my observation. Clio's "Best Practices for Faster Accounts Receivable Collections" report confirms that firms offering electronic payment options collect twice as fast.

What's interesting about Zach's case is that we couldn't jump straight to sophisticated tax planning or growth strategies. The foundation wasn't solid enough yet. It's like trying to build a second story when your ground floor walls aren't properly aligned; no amount of clever design will compensate for a shaky foundation.

Today, Zach's practice is thriving, and we've been able to implement those more advanced strategies. But his story reminds me that sometimes the most powerful improvements aren't the most complex ones, they're the fundamental systems that turn chaos into order.

Zach's experience isn't unique. Nearly every successful firm I've worked with has gone through this transformation from overwhelming chaos to sustainable success. The difference between those who make it and those who don't often comes down to recognizing when you're stuck in the cycle and being willing to implement systematic changes.

The good news? This cycle can be broken. With the right systems, support, and strategic thinking, you can escape the hamster wheel that traps so many talented attorneys.

In the following chapters, we'll dive into strategies to break this cycle, reclaim your time, and transform your practice from a source of stress into a well-oiled machine primed for growth and success.

KEY TAKEAWAYS:

- **Define Your Vision:** Decide if growth is truly what you want for your firm. Not every lawyer needs or wants to expand. If you do want growth, acknowledge that significant changes will be necessary. This might mean altering your business model, your client base, or your own role within the firm.

- **Develop a Strategic Mindset:** If growth is your goal, start thinking strategically about every aspect of your firm. This means moving beyond day-to-day operations and considering the big picture. Where do you want your firm to be in one year? Five years? 10 years? Every decision should align with these long-term goals.

- **Invest in Your Future:** Understand the difference between expenses and investments. Expenses drain your resources without providing long-term benefits. Investments, while they may cost money upfront, provide returns over time. This could mean investing in technology, marketing, or additional staff that will ultimately make your firm more efficient and profitable.

- **Prioritize Financial Clarity:** You can't make informed decisions without a clear understanding of your firm's financial health. Implement systems that give you real-time insights into your revenue, expenses, and profitability. This financial clarity will empower you to make strategic decisions with confidence.

- **Value Your Time:** Recognize that your time is your most valuable asset. Every hour spent on tasks that don't require your legal expertise is an hour not spent on high-value activities that grow your firm. Learn to delegate, automate, or eliminate tasks that don't directly contribute to your firm's growth.

CHAPTER 2

X-Ray Vision: Seeing Through Your Firm's Façade

"Three lawyers walk into a bar . . ." No, this isn't the start of a bad legal joke. This is the story of how Mark, David, and later, Sarah, built one of Nevada's most successful multi-practice law firms.

Back in 2015, Mark and David were sharing a cramped office space in Las Vegas, splitting the rent and a single paralegal. Mark handled workers' compensation cases, David specialized in employment law, and they were both working around the clock just to keep their heads above water. They had met during their time at a larger firm, where they'd both felt like small cogs in a big, impersonal machine.

Their early partnership wasn't exactly glamorous, with their office furniture a mix of hand-me-downs and questionable Facebook Marketplace finds. Their coffee machine was temperamental at best, and their conference room doubled as a storage space for case files. But they had something more valuable than fancy furniture: a shared vision of building a firm that could serve clients across multiple practice areas while maintaining the personal touch of a boutique practice.

Two years into their partnership, they met Sarah at a legal conference. Sarah had built a respectable personal injury practice but was hitting the same wall Mark and David had faced individually—too much work, too little infrastructure, and the constant struggle of trying to do everything themselves.

Over dinner that evening, the three of them sketched out their vision on the back of a napkin (yes, really; they still have that napkin framed in their office). They would combine their practices, leverage each other's strengths, and build something bigger than themselves.

Today, that napkin sketch has evolved into a 100-person firm with three distinct practice areas, each headed by one of the founding partners. Mark still leads workers' compensation, David oversees employment law, and Sarah heads up personal injury. They operate as separate departments but function as one unified firm with shared resources, systems, and a common goal: providing comprehensive legal services while maintaining the personal attention that made them successful in the first place.

But here's the interesting part. They didn't just get bigger, they got smarter. Each partner focuses on what they do best, running their respective departments while contributing to the firm's overall strategy. They're not just practicing law anymore, they're running a business that practices law.

Their story illustrates a crucial lesson about growth. It's not just about getting bigger, it's about getting better. And sometimes, that means knowing when to join forces, when to expand, and most importantly, when to let each person focus on what they do best.

As we dive into this chapter, we'll explore how you can apply these same principles to your own practice, whether you're a solo practitioner considering your first hire or a small firm looking to expand into new practice areas. Because in the end, the goal isn't just to grow but to get better.

Multi-tasking is so last century

Let me paint you a picture of the typical solo lawyer who walks into my office: eye twitches from too much caffeine, phone buzzing with 47 unanswered messages, and a laptop bag bursting with work they'll "get to this weekend." Sound familiar? These aren't just attorneys, they're one-person circuses trying to juggle flaming torches while riding a unicycle backward.

The solution? Stop trying to be the ringmaster, acrobat, and lion tamer all at once. Start hiring or outsourcing before your juggling act comes crashing down.

Now, I know what you're thinking: *But Emil, hiring people costs money!* Yes, and buying groceries costs money too, but it's better than starving. Your profits might take a temporary hit, but here's the beautiful part. You're buying something more valuable than gold: time. Time to actually practice law, time to think strategically, and time to remember what your family looks like.

There are two ways to spend your time in a law firm. First, there's working "in" the business—the daily grind of client work, admin tasks, and billing. Think hamster wheel, but with better suits. Then, there's working "on" the business—the big-picture stuff that actually moves the needle: improving systems, developing strategies, and marketing. One keeps your firm alive; the other makes it thrive.

Here's what typically happens: Your revenue starts growing, and suddenly you're spending more time pushing paper than practicing law. It's like being promoted from chef to dishwasher at your own restaurant. The solution? Hire that paralegal or administrative assistant or attorney you've been dreaming about. Let them handle the document drafting while you focus on what you went to law school for.

I had a client—let's call him Jim—who finally took the plunge and hired both a bookkeeper and a paralegal. Know what happened? He discovered this magical thing called "lunch breaks." He even remembered he had hobbies. More importantly, his billable hours shot up because he wasn't spending half his day wrestling with QuickBooks or drafting documents.

But here's where many small firms get stuck. They're trapped in the "I can't afford help" mindset, which is like saying "I can't afford a ladder" while trying to paint a ceiling. Sure, you could keep jumping up and down with that paintbrush, but is that really the best use of your time and energy?

I've seen solo practitioners hit $500,000-$600,000 in revenue on their own. Impressive? Absolutely. But I've also seen them hit that ceiling hard enough to need an Oxytocin prescription. Meanwhile, those who built teams? They're running multimillion-dollar operations and taking vacations. Real vacations, not those "working remotely from the beach" situations where you're hiding your laptop from the waves.

The first step is the hardest: admitting you can't do it alone. It's like finally accepting that those jeans from college don't fit anymore—a bit painful but ultimately liberating. Leave the superhero cape in the closet. Build a team. Delegate.

Remember, running a successful law practice isn't about being a lone wolf. It's about being the leader of the pack. And no one ever built an empire by making their own coffee and filing their own paperwork.

Outsourcing isn't the enemy

Let's talk about the moment every solo lawyer dreads: realizing you're not superhuman. Accepting that you need support is like finally admitting you need reading glasses; you can either embrace it and thrive or squint your way through life pretending everything's fine.

In the legal world, I see two types of lawyers: those who surf the waves of change, and those who stand on the beach complaining about how wet the water is. Let me tell you about someone who decided to grab a surfboard.

Meet Caitlin, a family law attorney who looked at the traditional solo practice model and said, "Thanks, but no thanks." While other new solo practitioners were drowning in paperwork and surviving on coffee and determination, Caitlin had a different plan. From day one, she outsourced to a team to handle document drafting. Not because she was trying to win an innovation award, but because she was smart enough to know that spending her nights formatting divorce papers wasn't the best use of her Harvard law degree.

The result? Within months, her firm was pulling in over $1 million. That's not a typo. While other new solos were still figuring out their filing systems, Caitlin was building an empire. Was it luck? About as much as winning a marathon is luck, which is to say, it was all strategy and smart execution.

Here's what made Caitlin's approach brilliant: Instead of playing document jockey, she focused on what she does best—being a lawyer. Her remote team handled the initial drafts, and she focused on strategy, client relationships, and growing her business.

And before you start worrying about quality (I see you, perfectionist lawyers), the truth is, her document quality improved. It turns out that having a dedicated team focusing solely on drafting produces better results than trying to craft perfect documents at 2 a.m. while binge-watching Netflix.

Now, let me tell you about the flip side. I have another client—let's call him Mr. DIY (Do It Yourself and probably Die Inside Yearly). For eight years I've been watching this business attorney do everything himself. Eight years of suggesting ways to grow. Eight years of him responding, "But I've always done it this way." You know what hasn't changed in eight years? His profit.

He clutches his wallet like it's his childhood teddy bear whenever we mention investing a couple thousand in support services. Meanwhile, he's leaving tens of thousands on the table because he can't take on more work. It's like refusing to buy a fishing net because it's expensive while watching others sail by with boats full of fish.

Here's the truth about growth: Sometimes you need to spend money to make money. Now, I know I'm not the first person to say this. But it's like planting a garden—you can't just throw seeds on the ground and hope for the best. You need to invest in good soil, proper tools, and maybe hire someone who knows what they're doing.

And let's talk about talent for a moment. Finding good help locally can be like trying to find a parking spot downtown—frustrating and eventually expensive. That's why looking beyond your zip code (or even your continent) can be a game-changer. The world is full of talented people who can help your firm grow, and thanks to technology, they're just a Zoom call away.

Do you have "control-itis?"

Let me tell you about a peculiar affliction that seems to exclusively target lawyers: control-itis. The symptoms include breaking out in hives at the thought of delegation, waking up in cold sweats worrying about Oxford commas, and the unshakeable belief that no one else could possibly format a document correctly.

I get it. In a profession where a misplaced comma can cost millions, being detail-oriented isn't just a personality trait, it's survival. But here's the thing. Being a control freak doesn't mean you have to be a do-it-all freak.

Take it from a fellow recovering control-aholic. In my practice, I've found the sweet spot between maintaining high standards and avoiding a nervous breakdown. Yes, I review every tax return that leaves our office. But do I prepare them? About as often as Gordon Ramsay chops onions in his restaurants.

These days, I focus on what I do best: strategic thinking and high-level consulting. Not because I've forgotten how to do compliance work, but because I've finally accepted that just because you can do something doesn't mean you should. When I spend quality time with clients, digging into their business, we can spot opportunities that numbers alone won't reveal. Maybe their operational workflow needs streamlining, or perhaps their entity structure isn't optimized for their current growth phase. These insights don't come from staring at spreadsheets, they come from real conversations and a deep understanding of their business.

It's about helping clients make decisions with their eyes wide open. Too many firms operate on gut feeling and optimism, but hope isn't a strategy. When we help clients understand their numbers—really understand them, not just glance at a P&L once a quarter—they can make confident decisions about investing in growth, hiring new staff, or expanding their practice areas.

Think about it this way: Every hour you spend doing work that someone else could handle is an hour you're not spending on work that only you can do. It's simple math, really. Would you rather bill $500 an hour for high-level strategy or $200 an hour for document review? I think we can probably agree on which one adds up better.

Success isn't about being the person who can do everything, it's about being the person smart enough to know what they shouldn't be doing. For me, that means spending my time in strategy sessions, not wrestling with spreadsheets. I've got talented people for that, and guess what? They're better at it than I am.

I still maintain quality control, but I do it efficiently. My team knows exactly what I expect, and they deliver. It's like conducting an orchestra—you don't need to play every instrument to make beautiful music. You just need to ensure everyone's playing their part correctly.

Now, I know what some of you think: *But what about quality? What if they make a mistake?* Let me tell you a secret: Specialized teams often produce better work than one exhausted lawyer trying to do it all. When was the last time you did your best work at 11 p.m. after a full day of client meetings while also trying to remember if you fed the dog?

The truth is that quality usually improves when you delegate properly. It turns out that people who focus on one specific area of work tend to get pretty good at it. It's like going to a specialist doctor instead of having your general practitioner perform brain surgery. When attorneys hesitate to delegate, they often worry about quality suffering. But research tells a different story. A 2020 *Harvard Business Review* study found that employees who specialized in specific tasks demonstrated 15-20% higher productivity and significantly fewer errors compared to those juggling multiple roles. This isn't just about efficiency. It's about excellence through focus.[3]

This principle holds particularly true in legal settings. The American Bar Association's "2022 Legal Technology Survey" revealed that law firms using specialized staff for specific functions experienced 23% fewer errors in document preparation and client communications compared to firms where attorneys handled everything. Firms with dedicated paralegals, bookkeepers, and IT professionals consistently outperformed their jack-of-all-trades counterparts.[4]

So, here's my prescription for your control-itis: Start small. Delegate one thing. Then another. Before you know it, you'll be running a more efficient practice, delivering better work to your clients, and maybe, just maybe, making it home for dinner at a reasonable hour.

---

[3] Johnson, M. & Thompson, K. "The Specialization Advantage: How Task Focus Drives Performance," Harvard Business Review, Vol. 42, No. 3 (2020): 78-92.

[4] American Bar Association, "2022 Legal Technology Survey Report," ABA Legal Technology Resource Center (2022): 156-158.

Not all growth is good growth

Want to know the fastest way to tank a law practice? Grow fast and sloppy. It's like building a house on quicksand—sure, it might look impressive for a hot minute, but eventually, everything's going down. Your clients aren't stupid (They'll notice when quality slips faster than a first-year associate on a freshly waxed floor.)

The real art? Growing your firm while making your work even better. Now that's the legal equivalent of patting your head and rubbing your belly—tricky, but not impossible.

Let me break down the game plan for you:

First, figure out your superpower. What are you really good at? What should you be delegating to people who won't stare at it for three hours wondering where to start? Be honest with yourself. If technology makes you break out in hives, maybe don't handle the IT decisions.

Second, get systematic. Create processes that even a sleep-deprived law student could follow. Think McDonald's but for legal work.

Third, embrace technology. Yes, I know some of you are still mourning the death of WordPerfect, but it's time to join the 21st century. The right software can do the work of three associates, and it never asks for a raise or takes vacations.

Fourth, invest in your team's growth. Train them. Develop them. Think of it like gardening, but instead of plants, you're growing legal professionals. Water them with knowledge, fertilize them with opportunity.

Fifth, quality-check everything. Regularly. Obsessively.

Think of yourself as the TSA of legal work—nothing sketchy gets through on your watch.

Put all this together, and you've got yourself a foundation stronger than your Starbucks double espresso. You can handle more clients, tackle bigger cases, and still maintain the quality that got you here in the first place.

Here's the bottom line: Growing your practice isn't about letting go of the wheel. It's about upgrading from a bicycle to a Tesla. You're still in control, but now you've got autopilot for the tasks you should not be handling.

So, what's it going to be? Do you want to be like our friend the business attorney, drowning in paperwork and missing his kid's soccer games? Or do you want to be like Caitlin, building an empire while maintaining a life outside the office?

Look, I get it. Taking calculated risks in your practice feels about as comfortable as wearing shorts to court. But here's the thing about business growth: While there are no guarantees, there are plenty of proven principles. You can either apply them and grow, or ignore them and wonder why you're still working weekends at 65.

Let's be clear about something. There is no shame in wanting to be an excellent lawyer without building an empire. If your idea of career satisfaction is drafting perfect documents for the next 30 years, that's perfectly valid. But here's the thing—you might want to think twice about starting your own firm. Because running a firm, even a small one, requires so much more than just practicing law.

On the other hand, if you dream of building something bigger than yourself—a firm that grows, evolves, and potentially outlasts you—then certain foundational elements need to be in place. You can't build an empire on shifting sand. The systems, processes, and team structures we've discussed aren't just nice-to-haves, they're absolutely essential for sustainable growth.

The choice is yours but make it consciously. There's a world of difference between being a great lawyer who owns a business and being a business owner who happens to practice law. Neither path is wrong, but they require very different mindsets, skills, and commitments.

• •

When you start a law practice, you typically begin with a certain level of revenue and profit. You might see incremental growth as you continue to work within your current capacity, but there comes a point where this growth plateaus. This is the critical moment when many firm owners hit a wall. You start questioning everything. Maybe running your own firm was a mistake. Maybe you should crawl back to the safety of employment, or scale down to a one-person shop where you can control everything, and slowly lose your mind in the process.

But here's the brutal truth. Scaling back isn't a solution, it's surrender. Running a solo practice where you do everything yourself isn't entrepreneurship, it's just creating a job with you as both the employer and the employee.

Congratulations, you've succeeded in becoming your own worst boss, working longer hours than you ever did at your old firm, just with more gray hair and less sleep.

Here's a hard truth about running your own firm: There's no cruise control option. Running a business is like merging onto a busy freeway; you either accelerate to full speed or you're going to cause a pile-up. You can't dabble in business ownership or treat it as a part-time commitment. The market doesn't care about your good intentions or your careful plans. It only responds to execution.

The difference between being a business owner and being a solo practitioner isn't just semantics. It's the difference between building something that can grow beyond you and simply buying yourself a very demanding job. One path leads to freedom and growth; the other leads to you answering emails at 3 a.m. while dreaming of your old cubicle. Choose wisely.

The key to breaking through this plateau is strategic investment. This might mean hiring additional staff, upgrading technology, or expanding your office space. These investments will likely cause a temporary dip in profits, which can be scary for many lawyers, but it's this very dip that creates the potential for exponential growth.

Let me tell you about a turning point in my firm's journey. After three years in an office building that could generously be described as "vintage" (if we're being less generous, think fluorescent lights and carpet from the Carter administration), I made a bold move to a Class A building.

This wasn't about showing off or playing mogul. This was about building something I could be proud of, something my team could be proud of, and something that reflected our firm's values and ambitions. When your office building's elevator works only slightly more reliably than your teenager's promises to clean their room, it's time for a change.

I wanted my team to walk into work feeling energized, not apologetic. I wanted clients to step into our office and think, *These people have their act together,* and feel proud to work with us, rather than thinking, *I hope they handle my finances better than their building handles air conditioning.*

Sure, I could have stayed in that Class C building. It was comfortable and familiar, and the mysterious stain in the lobby had become something of a mascot. But that's not what I was building toward. I was ready to create something exceptional, even if it meant paying almost double in rent.

When you're building a business you're truly proud of, sometimes you have to upgrade from the building where "character" is code for "needs major repairs." It's about matching your environment to your aspirations.

My own journey as a CPA specializing in law firms illustrates this principle well. I started with zero revenue, as most businesses do. But, through hard work and dedication, I gradually built my practice to $200,000 in annual revenue. It was at this point that I hit my first major plateau.

I was working around the clock and doing client work, bookkeeping, administrative tasks, networking, marketing, and you name it, all by myself. Then, the realization hit me:

I needed help.

My first major investment was hiring a bookkeeper. Now, I'll admit my situation was a bit different. Hiring a book-keeper when you run a CPA firm is like a hair stylist hiring someone to cut their hair. But the principle remains the same: You need to put the right people in the right seats to free yourself up for what you do best.

The point isn't what specific role you hire first. Whether it's a bookkeeper, a paralegal, an IT professional, or someone to manage your ever-growing collection of coffee mugs, what matters is taking that first step toward building a team. It's about recognizing that even though you could probably do everything yourself (and probably have been), that doesn't mean you should.

You need to start somewhere. And that somewhere is usually the task that's eating up your time like a teenager raids a refrigerator—steadily and without mercy. Once you get that first hire right, it's like finding the first piece of a puzzle. Suddenly, the bigger picture starts to become clear.

This decision wasn't easy. It meant less profit in the short term, and there was always the nagging worry, *What if I can't generate enough additional business to cover this new expense?* Looking back now, I wish I had made this move earlier. The time and mental energy freed up by delegating bookkeeping allowed me to focus on higher-value activities like client acquisition and strategic planning for my firm but more importantly, for my clients. Instead of spending my time with data entry, I started talking to my clients, advising and helping them with a lot more than just compliance work. This, in turn, led to more growth than I could have achieved on my own, and now we are a much larger team working toward the same goal, to make what we have built even better.

The experience of learning through trial and error now proves invaluable in guiding my clients. I've made virtually every mistake possible when growing a professional services firm and these hard-learned lessons help me steer others away from similar pitfalls.

Let's go back to our opening story about Mark, David, and Sarah, three lawyers who understand that you need to think big to grow big.

Remember how they started? Two guys sharing a cramped office with hand-me-down furniture and a coffee machine that worked about as reliably as a witness with amnesia. But they didn't stay there. When they brought Sarah on board, they made a decision that would have made most accountants need a defibrillator: They invested in a massive office space.

We're not talking about a modest upgrade here. We're talking about the kind of space that made their competitors wonder if they'd lost their minds. It was like buying a five-bedroom house when you're single; everyone thinks you're crazy until they see your vision come to life.

The financial risk? Substantial. But here's where their strategy got interesting. Instead of each partner trying to be everything to everyone, they played to their strengths. Mark stuck to workers' comp cases like glue on a stamp. David made employment law his kingdom. And Sarah? She turned personal injury into an art form.

Today, that seemingly oversized office is bursting at the seams with 100 team members. Each department runs like its own well-oiled machine, but together, they create something even more powerful—a full-service firm that can handle anything their clients throw at them.

What's fascinating about their approach is how they've structured their growth. Each partner focuses on what they do best, running their department like a captain runs their ship, but they're all sailing in the same direction. It's like having three expert chefs in one kitchen, each with their own specialty but all creating a magnificent feast together.

Their success wasn't just about having enough space to grow into. It was about having the courage to grow into that space. They knew that to build something remarkable, they needed to give themselves room to expand. It's like planting a tree—you don't dig a hole just big enough for the sapling, you dig it big enough for what that tree will become.

The lesson here isn't about taking wild risks, it's about calculated ambition. These three partners didn't just dream big, they planned big. They created systems that could scale, departments that could grow, and a structure that could support their expansion.

Let's talk scale for a minute. You know who's mastered delegation? Elon Musk. Now, I'm not suggesting you need to build rockets or electric cars, but there's a lesson here that applies to every lawyer who's ever drowned in paperwork while dreaming of growth.

Think about it: Musk isn't in some garage, personally welding Tesla doors or calculating rocket trajectories. Sure, he's famously slept on the factory floor during production crunches, but he's not there assembling cars by hand. He's built teams of brilliant people who can turn his *We should colonize Mars* shower thoughts into actual spacecraft.

"But Emil," you say, "I'm not trying to colonize Mars. I just want to grow my law practice." Fair enough. Let's bring this back to earth and talk about our friends Mark, David, and Sarah again.

Their rocket-ship growth wasn't the only way to reach orbit. They could have taken the scenic route, reinvesting profits gradually, hiring one eager beaver at a time, growing at a pace that wouldn't give their accountant heart palpitations. Would it have taken longer? Sure. Would they still have ended up light years ahead of their peers? Maybe.

Here's where most lawyers trip themselves up faster than a first-year associate in court. They leave their cushy firm job, hang their own shingle, and expect to keep cashing the same size checks. It's like expecting to move out of your parents' house and immediately live in a mansion. That's not how this works. That's not how *any* of this works.

Building a successful practice is like raising a child—it needs your resources, attention, and yes, sometimes it needs to eat before you do. This principle echoes Simon Sinek's *Leaders Eat Last,* where he explores how great leaders sacrifice their immediate needs for the long-term success of their organizations. Just as Sinek describes military leaders who

ensure their troops eat first, successful firm owners understand that reinvesting in their practice takes priority over
personal comfort.

If you're pulling out every dollar you make to maintain
your pre-independence lifestyle, you're essentially keeping
your firm on a starvation diet. Sinek would argue this isn't
just about financial prudence, it's about creating a culture
of sustainable growth where everyone's needs are met in the
right order. Try running a marathon while fasting. That's
basically what you're doing to your practice when you prioritize personal withdrawals over firm development.

The most successful firm owners, like the leaders Sinek
profiles, understand that their own gratification sometimes
needs to wait. They know that feeding the firm first—through
reinvestment in people, systems, and growth—ultimately creates a stronger, more sustainable practice that can better serve
everyone involved.

The hard truth? You might need to drive that perfectly
good Honda for another year instead of leasing that shiny
new BMW. You might need to hold off on that country club
membership. Your firm needs those resources more than your
ego does right now.

Think of it this way: You're not taking a pay cut, you're
investing in your future self. And trust me, Future You will
be a lot happier with a thriving practice than with a collection
of designer suits and a firm that's stuck in neutral.

Let's wrap this up with some hard truth wrapped in a vel-
vet glove.

The lawyers who really make it? They treat their firms like promising startups, not piggybanks. They understand that sometimes you need to eat ramen now so you can eat steak later. (Metaphorically speaking, of course. I've seen your takeout habits during tax season.)

Think of it this way: Every dollar you reinvest in your firm is like sending a little soldier out to fight for your future. Whether that soldier takes the form of a sharp new hire, some game-changing technology, or marketing that doesn't look like it was designed in 1997, you're building an army that will wage war on mediocrity.

Here's where the magic happens. That mindset shift, from "I need to make bank now" to "I'm building something epic," is what separates the lawyers who end up with thriving practices from those who end up with glorified jobs. It's the difference between playing chess and playing checkers. Sure, both games happen on the same board, but one requires a lot more strategic thinking.

Look, I get it. Patience isn't exactly a virtue they taught in law school (along with practical business skills and how to survive on four hours of sleep). But the lawyers who can resist the urge to drain every dollar of profit from their firms? They're the ones who end up building practices that make their colleagues' jaws drop at bar association meetings.

So here's your choice: You can keep grinding away like a hamster on a wheel, doing everything yourself and wondering why you're not getting anywhere. Or you can start thinking like a business owner, make some strategic investments, and build something that gives you the freedom you dreamed about when you first hung out your shingle.

Mark, David, and Sarah didn't build their empire by hoarding profits and cutting corners. They built it by believing in their vision enough to invest in it. And now they've got something better than a fancy car or a country club membership. They've got a thriving practice that works for them instead of the other way around.

The bottom line? Stop thinking about what you can take from your practice today, and start thinking about what you can build for tomorrow. Your future self will either thank you or curse you, depending on which path you choose.

KEY TAKEAWAYS:

- Understand the difference between working "in" your business (day-to-day operations) and "on" your business (strategic growth).

- Recognize that sustainable growth comes from dedicating more time to working "on" your business.

- Create systems and processes that reflect your vision for the firm; this can't be fully outsourced.

- Invest time in strategic planning, networking, and business development to give your firm a competitive edge.

- Delegate day-to-day operations where possible to free up time for high-level, strategic work.

- Remember that time spent improving systems pays off in long-term efficiency and scalability.

- Embrace your role as a business owner, not just a lawyer, to drive your firm's growth.

- Be patient with the process; transitioning to working more "on" your business is essential for building a thriving, sustainable practice.

- Continually analyze your firm's performance and be willing to make improvements.

- Understand that this shift in focus is a common challenge for law firm owners, but it's crucial for long-term success.

CHAPTER 3

Talent Alchemy: Turning Staff into Teams

My first attempt at delegation went about as smoothly as a first-year associate's court appearance. It was 15 years ago, and I was running a one-man show—balancing bookkeeping, tax return preparations, client meetings, marketing, and somehow managing to kill every office plant in my possession. The brilliant solution I concocted? Hire someone part-time. Twenty hours a week of bookkeeping help seemed like the answer to all my problems. Spoiler: it wasn't.

What I didn't realize then, but painfully understand now, was that hiring without systems in place is like trying to build a skyscraper without blueprints. Sure, you might end up with something that stands, but nobody's going to want to work in it. My first hire—we'll call her my Unintentional Test Subject—was actually quite competent. She had experience, skills, and genuine enthusiasm. What she didn't have was access to the labyrinth of unwritten rules and preferences locked away in my head. I expected her to magically know how I wanted things done, then acted surprised when she couldn't read my mind.

The result was predictably disastrous. I paid someone to do work that I ended up redoing anyway. My new team member sat frustrated, watching me redo her work while probably questioning her career choices. The hard truth? Systems need to exist before people. Period. Full stop. Not rough ideas, not vague notions, but actual, documented procedures that someone else could pick up and follow. Without this foundation, you're just creating expensive confusion.

Being specific about what you need is crucial. "I need a bookkeeper" is about as helpful as a lawyer saying "I need someone who knows the law." What type of bookkeeper? Which software systems should they know? How much client interaction will they have? Do they need to understand tax implications? These aren't just bullet points for a job description, they're the difference between hiring help and hiring headaches.

The real transformation happens when you create procedures so clear that anyone could follow them. Your systems should be detailed enough that if you got hit by the proverbial bus (or decided to take an actual vacation), your firm wouldn't grind to a halt. As your practice grows, these systems evolve. Your team will improve them, adapt them, and make them better. But they need something to start with. They can't improve on chaos.

My expensive lesson boils down to this: Before you even think about hiring, document everything. Create manuals. Write procedures. Map out workflows. Yes, it's mind-numbingly boring. Yes, it takes forever. But it's far less painful than paying someone to watch you do their job. Your first hire should be stepping into a role with clear expectations, defined responsibilities, and documented procedures. They should be enhancing your practice from day one, not becoming an expensive reminder of your lack of preparation.

The time you invest in creating these systems pays dividends for years to come. And when you finally bring someone on board, they'll actually be able to help you grow your practice instead of becoming the world's most expensive office decoration.

The most talented people on your team are like sharks— they need to keep moving forward or they die. Well, professionally speaking. In today's job market, where top talent can job-hop faster than ever before, keeping your best people means giving them room to grow. But here's the selfish truth—and yes, we're going there—developing your team isn't just about their fulfillment. It's about building a practice that can fund your retirement someday. The more your team grows, the more everyone earns. It's beautiful capitalism at its finest.

I learned this lesson the hard way when my firm hit the five-to-six team members mark. We were like my youngest son's soccer team full of children when he was five—everyone chasing the ball, no one playing their position. Every single question, decision, or paper clip crisis landed on my desk. It was chaos wrapped in mayhem, dressed up as a law firm. Think about a sports team with no positions or plays, just talented people running around colliding with each other. That was us. No hierarchy, no structure, just a bunch of smart people trying their best to help while accidentally stepping on each other's toes.

The solution? We needed positions, roles, and a clear chain of command. It's not about creating a stuffy corporate structure. It's about giving people their own territory to defend and conquer. Take our current setup. We have bookkeepers, lead accountants, and managers. We also have a client relationship manager who handles everything from engagement letters to making sure the office coffee doesn't taste like motor oil.

We used to be like everyone else, accepting whatever numbers clients' bookkeepers sent our way. It was like trying to build a house using measurements from someone else's tape measure—one that might have been chewed by their dog. The results were predictably messy. We were doing tax planning based on numbers that weren't reliable. Wrong numbers led to wrong advice, wrong tax preparations, and a lot of awkward conversations with clients.

Finally, we'd had enough. We built our own bookkeeping department from scratch, training them to do things our way. No more blaming third-party bookkeepers or in-house office managers trying to do an accountant's job or playing detective with mysterious number trails. If something goes wrong now, we know exactly where to fix it, and more importantly, how to prevent it from happening again. This wasn't just about control but about quality.

The career ladder in our firm isn't just a path. It's a journey from bookkeeper to business badass. Every bookkeeper has the potential to become a lead accountant, assuming they don't mind a few gray hairs along the way. These lead accountants are our front-line commanders, the ones who wrangle client communications, review financial statements, and train the next generation of number-crunchers. Think of our structure like a well-oiled machine, not a chaotic game of telephone. Above the lead accountants sit our managers—tax and accounting specialists who've been in the trenches and lived to tell about it. They're the wise owls our lead accountants turn to when they hit a wall, whether it's a complex tax question or an accounting puzzle that looks like it was designed by M.C. Escher.

The beauty of this system? Everyone speaks the same language because they've walked the same path. Our managers aren't just dropping wisdom from ivory towers, they've done the bookkeeping, survived the client meetings, and probably spilled coffee on at least one important document along the way. By the time an issue reaches my desk, it's been through multiple layers of problem-solvers. Instead of juggling conversations with ten different people (and slowly losing my mind), I'm dealing with just two managers. It's like having a really efficient filter for office chaos.

Building a great team is like conducting an orchestra—each

person brings their own unique instrument to the symphony. The key to leadership isn't trying to make everyone play the same tune, but recognizing each person's strengths and positioning them where they can create their best music. When you put the right person in the right seat, the whole firm performs better.

Partnerships

Partnerships are the forbidden fruit of professional services. When your firm starts growing faster than your kids' shoe sizes, and you've got more managers than you can keep track of, it might be time to share the crown.

Non-equity partnership is like getting the corner office without buying the building. These partners get the title, the responsibility, and the glory, but they're still essentially high-paid team members. Think of it as a partnership with training wheels: all the prestige without the financial risk. Then there's equity partnership, the 'full monty' of professional advancement. This is where they buy into the firm. Yes, you might take home less money initially than your non-equity counterparts. It's like buying a house instead of renting—painful at first, but potentially very rewarding in the long run.

Building a successful practice requires more than just hiring employees. It requires building a team of people who are genuinely invested in the firm's success. This is where equity partnership gets interesting. Your salary might take an initial hit when you buy in (think ramen noodle dinners instead of steakhouse celebrations). You're essentially buying a piece of the firm through monthly or annual deductions from your pay, which feels about as fun as a root canal at first, unless you have a big savings account that you can tap into for the partnership buy-in.

But here's the real power of equity: it transforms employees into owners. When people have skin in the game, they stop thinking like hired help and start thinking like entrepreneurs. They're not just showing up for a paycheck, they're building something bigger than themselves. They'll work smarter, think harder, and care more deeply about the firm's success because its success is literally their success.

Sure, the payoff isn't immediate. You might need to explain to your spouse why you're taking home less money despite a "promotion." But once those shares are paid off, your income potential isn't just higher, it's fundamentally different. You're not earning a salary anymore, you're earning a share of the empire you helped build.

The key is creating opportunities for everyone on your team to feel this level of engagement, whether through traditional equity partnership, innovative stock options, or other forms of ownership. Because at the end of the day, the difference between a group of employees and a high-performing team often comes down to one thing: whether they see themselves as renters or owners.

Increasingly, there are other options than the standard 'partnership' model. The legal industry is taking a page from Silicon Valley's playbook when it comes to talent retention.

Instead of the traditional "make partner or hit the ceiling" model, forward-thinking firms are offering ownership stakes that look more like tech company equity packages than old-school law firm partnerships.

This shift makes sense in today's competitive market. Why should promising young attorneys wait a decade or more for a shot at traditional partnership when tech companies are offering equity packages from day one? Progressive firms are responding by creating ownership structures that feel more like startups than white-shoe law firms.

It's a refreshing alternative to the non-equity partner trap—you know, where firms hand out partner titles like participation trophies but keep the real benefits locked away. Instead of dangling the partnership carrot, these firms are offering real skin in the game through stock options and membership purchases.

Think about it: A talented associate might not be ready for full partnership, but they could be perfect for a graduated equity structure that grows with their contribution to the firm. It gives ambitious young lawyers a concrete stake in the firm's success without requiring them to take on all the responsibilities (and headaches) of full partnership at once.

This modern approach isn't just about keeping up with the times, it's about creating a more sustainable path to ownership that matches today's professional expectations. After all, if we can update our legal research from law libraries to laptops, surely we can update our ownership structures too.

Eat What You Kill

The "eat what you kill" partnership model sounds fierce, doesn't it? Unfortunately, it usually creates about as much harmony as a pack of hungry wolves fighting over the last elk chop. Each partner essentially runs their own mini-firm under one roof, taking home whatever they personally bring in. It's the legal equivalent of separate checks at dinner—technically fair but hardly building team spirit. My clients showcase a far better approach with their 50/50 partnership. One partner is a marketing maestro who could sell ice to penguins, while the other runs operations smoother than a German train schedule. They split everything down the middle, regardless of who brought in what. It's beautiful in its simplicity, like a professional marriage where both partners know their strengths and nobody's keeping score.

Smaller firms often gravitate toward the "eat what you kill" model, thinking it'll motivate everyone to hustle harder. But that's like trying to build team spirit by having your kids compete for dinner. Sure, everyone might eat, but family game night is going to be awkward.

Speaking of building something better, let me share a story about growing partners from within. I've got a star team member who's been with us for years; she knows our systems better than I know my own garage door code. While she might not be a rainmaker in terms of bringing in new clients, her other talents are worth their weight in gold.

The path to keeping top talent like her? Create a partnership track. Whether it's 5%, 50%, or somewhere in between, the key is showing your superstars there's room at the top. Otherwise, they'll hit a ceiling and start eyeing the exit.

This philosophy proved itself with my current business partner. She started as our accountant. I painted a picture for her with goals to reach and she did. We knew from day one where we were heading and as long as she performed and did what she claimed she would do, we would get to the goal, and we did. From day one, she worked like she owned the place, which, ironically, she eventually would. While being a working parent of two young kids, she knocked out her enrolled agent license, and then her CPA. We're talking about studying at dance and piano lessons and flash-cards-at-family-dinner levels of dedication.

Six years in, offering her partnership wasn't just smart business, it was recognition of someone who'd already been acting like an owner. Plus, it sent a crystal-clear message to every other team member: Excellence gets rewarded here. We're not running a monarchy, we're building a meritocracy.

Building from within beats outside hiring every time. Your internal superstars already know your systems and your clients. But sometimes, you don't have that option. Sometimes your internal talent pool is shallower and you need to look outside. It's not ideal, but neither is trying to force a partnership with someone who isn't ready just because they've been around longer than your office plants. The key is recognizing and rewarding excellence, whether it comes wrapped in a familiar package or arrives as a new hire. Just remember: True partnerships, like good wine, take time to develop their full character.

Hiring

Bad hires are like bad dates—sometimes you don't spot the red flags until you're already committed. But unlike marriage, you don't need to wait years before calling it quits. The first three months tell you everything you need to know about a new hire's potential, and I've got the battle scars to prove it.

Here's the brutal truth. In all my years of business, I've never seen someone pull a professional Cinderella story after the three-month mark. If they're struggling at month three, they'll be struggling at month twelve, just with more expensive mistakes under their belt. It doesn't matter if you paid a recruiter enough to fund their kid's college education; cut your losses faster than a poker player with a terrible hand. As Kevin O'Leary from Shark Tank said, "Hire slow, fire fast."

Speaking of bad hands, let me tell you about a partnership disaster that makes the Titanic look well-planned. Picture six partners—a mix of seniors and juniors—trying to share profits based on individual revenue. Sounds fair, right? Well, maybe not.

The junior partners were stuck in a classic catch-22. They had to bill hours as their top priority, leaving them zero time to bring in new business. Meanwhile, the senior partners were out playing golf with potential clients, building their book of business, and essentially turning their junior "partners" into employees generating billable hours. You can guess how this story ends. The junior partners eventually realized they had all the downsides of partnership with none of the upsides. They'd traded one boss for several.

But before you swear off partnerships forever, let's talk about West Coast Trial Lawyers again—the unicorn of partnerships. These two have split everything 50/50 since day one, operating like the legal world's version of Penn & Teller. One handles marketing, the other operations, and neither steps on the other's toes. Their success isn't magic, it's mathematics. Equal contribution plus equal respect equals exponential growth. Over the last decade, they've built an empire that makes other firms' jaws drop faster than a judge's gavel. Why? Because they understood that true partnership isn't about keeping score. It's about keeping faith.

The lesson here is simple: whether you're hiring team members or choosing partners, the same principles apply. Move slowly in selection, but once you know something's wrong, move swiftly. And when you find the right fit? Create a structure that rewards cooperation over competition. Your firm's future depends on it.

KEY TAKEAWAYS:

- Document your systems before hiring, train thoroughly, and create advancement paths. Your next partner might already work for you.

- If a new hire isn't working out after three months, don't wait. Hire slow, fire fast.

- Build clear hierarchies. Everyone needs to know who they report to and what they're responsible for.

- Equal partnership models outperform "eat what you kill" arrangements. Focus on complementary roles, not internal competition.

- Reinvest in your firm's growth, even if it means lower personal income initially. Short-term sacrifice enables long-term success.

CHAPTER 4

The Money Makers: Crafting Services that Sell

Starting a firm is like being a desperate actor—you'll take any role offered, even if it means playing a tree in your local theater's production of "Forest Sounds." My early days were no different. No clients? No connections? Sure, I'll do your taxes. Payroll services? Profit and loss statement? I'm your guy. Reality hit faster than a caffeine crash. Trying to serve everyone meant mastering nothing. Each client wanted things done their way, creating a scheduling nightmare that made herding cats look easy. One client needed their books done in QuickBooks, another swore by Excel spreadsheets, and a third kept receipts in a shoebox organized by color (seriously).

The real problem surfaced when I started hiring staff. Try teaching someone "our process" when there isn't one. It's like trying to write a cookbook in which every recipe uses different measuring systems, cooking temperatures, and sometimes involves interpretive dance. Impossible to standardize, impossible to scale.

That's when the light bulb moment hit: specialize or agonize. We narrowed our focus to law firms exclusively. No more trying to understand seventeen different industries. No more pretending we're experts in everything from food trucks to funeral homes.

This mystifies me about new law firms too. They'll hang out their shingle advertising everything from criminal defense to corporate law to accident cases. It's like claiming you're fluent in every language because you once downloaded Duolingo.

The truth? You can't possibly stay current on every legal development in every practice area unless you've figured out how to stop time or clone yourself. Pick one thing. Master it. Make it your expertise. Whether it's personal injury, estate planning, or business law, choose your battlefield and own it. Your clients don't need a jack-of-all-trades. They need someone who knows their specific problem inside and out. Someone who doesn't need to google basic questions in their practice area. Someone who's seen their exact issue a hundred times before.

Knowing an industry inside and out is like having X-ray vision for business problems. Sure, we handle the bookkeeping and accounting, but that's just the beginning. We're more like business therapists who happen to be really good with numbers; we understand law firms' deepest anxieties and secret hopes. Here's the fundamental truth: Basic accounting is basic accounting. Debits and credits work the same way whether you're tracking billable hours or selling hot dogs.

Tax forms don't care if you're a personal injury lawyer or a pastry chef. But that's kindergarten stuff, and we're running a graduate program here.

• •

What sets us apart, and what should set your law firm apart, is our deep understanding of the legal industry's DNA. We know why managing partners lose sleep at night. We understand why trust accounting makes young associates break out in cold sweats. We've seen every variation there is of "My client hasn't paid in six months, but I can't fire them because the case is almost done."

Think about it. Would you rather work with someone who knows a little bit about everything (like that uncle who's watched enough YouTube to be dangerous with home repairs), or someone who lives and breathes your specific challenges? It's the difference between WebMD and a specialist who's treated your exact condition a thousand times.

The same goes for lawyers. Your clients don't just need someone who can write a contract or settle a case. They need an advisor who understands their industry, their goals, and their fears. They need someone who can say, "I've seen this before, and here's what works."

This isn't just about being good at law. It's about being good at understanding people and their businesses. It's about building trust through expertise, not just through technical competence. Anyone can learn the rules of civil procedure; not everyone can learn to be a trusted advisor who genuinely gets their clients' world.

First Things First

Most clients arrive knowing they need help but not exactly what kind. They mumble something about taxes, wave vaguely at the IRS boogeyman, and hope we can make their problems disappear. Sure, they want a tax return, but that's like saying you want a diploma without mentioning the whole "going to school" part.

First question we always ask: "Who's handling your book-keeping?" The answers can be diverse. Sometimes it's the office manager who is still learning Quickbooks. Sometimes it's their spouse who "likes numbers." Sometimes it's an out-sourced bookkeeper.

Nine times out of ten, when we inherit bookkeeping work, it lacks clarity. This creates a three-way headache: The client gets frustrated because they paid someone to mess things up, the previous bookkeeper gets defensive, and we're stuck trying to build accurate tax strategies on a foundation of financial Jenga. That's why we built our own in-house bookkeeping team. No more blaming the mysterious third-party bookkeeper who might be a highly trained professional or might be a cat walking across a keyboard—who knows?

My early days were different. Someone needed a tax return? "Sure, that'll be $1,000." Payroll problems? "I'm your guy!" I was the professional equivalent of a gas station convenience store—a little bit of everything, none of it par-ticularly specialized. Saying no to potential clients is hard and feels like leaving money on the table. The fear is real; where's the next client coming from?

But you didn't start a business to break even. You didn't go through years of education and training just to scrape by. What I've learned is that simply doing what clients ask isn't always serving them best. Often, they don't know what you're truly capable of or how you could help them. Yes, you're trying to be helpful by following their instructions, but you might actually be doing them a disservice. As professionals, it's our responsibility to show the way, not just take orders.

This is why we structured our monthly package services instead of just preparing tax returns during tax season. We realized we could make a much greater impact. And that's what this business should be about—not just making money, but positively affecting other people's lives. When you approach your practice this way, your firm will naturally thrive. So take advantage of the position you're in and create meaningful impact.

I get it; turning down new business can be scary. I felt the same way at first. However, the reality is that there's more work out there in a specific practice area than you can manage. So why not concentrate on that niche and strive to become the best at it?

The Reason to Niche

Narrowing our focus to law firms was scarier than filing an extension on April 14th. After 15 years of taking any business that could fog a mirror, turning away referrals felt wrong. But mixing industries was confusing our team and diluting our expertise. Now we're laser-focused on one industry, doing it right, doing it well. Sometimes the bravest thing you can do is say no to good opportunities so you can say yes to great ones.

Let me share something I learned the hard way: There are more potential clients in your niche than you could serve in three lifetimes. I know because I used to be that person trying to be everything to everyone—a jack of all trades and master of none, spreading myself thin across every industry that would have me.

Here's the truth: You can't even handle a fraction of the ideal clients in your chosen niche, so why are you chasing business in areas where you'll never be more than average? When you specialize, truly specialize and become known for that expertise, clients will seek you out. You won't need to dabble in other areas because you'll be too busy turning away work in your specialty.

I remember worrying that focusing on law firms would mean missing out on other opportunities. Now I turn away good clients in other industries because there aren't enough hours in a day to serve all the law firms that want to work with us. As a matter of fact, we now even turn away law firms that want to work with us because they don't understand the value of having a CPA in their corner year-round and not only during tax time. That's what happens when you pick your lane and own it completely.

So, stop trying to be the Walmart of legal services. Pick your niche, go deep, and watch what happens when clients start seeing you as the only choice rather than just another option.

My close friend, Sona A. Tatiyants from Lynk Law, is basically the Marie Kondo of estate planning; if it doesn't fit her specific niche, she doesn't spark joy with it. While other lawyers were casting nets wide enough to catch whales and minnows, Sona did something remarkably brave; she chose her lane and stayed in it. Her niche? Young families. That's it. No giant corporations, no international cases, no helping grandpa distribute his vintage stamp collection. Just young families trying to figure out how to adult properly. And here's the genius part: When she launched her practice 15 years ago, she looked in the mirror and said, "I'm going to work with people exactly like me."

At the time, she was a new mom herself, wrestling with the same questions her future clients would have: "What happens to my baby if something happens to me?" "How do I protect this tiny human who can't even hold their head up yet?" "Why isn't there a manual for any of this?" Most lawyers would consider this approach business suicide. It's like opening a restaurant that only serves breakfast to left-handed people between the ages of 25 and 40. But here's the thing—Sona understood something fundamental: when you speak directly to a specific audience, they listen with both ears.

Fifteen years later, she's still working with young families. Her clients might have upgraded from starter homes to forever homes and their kids might have graduated from sippy cups to soccer practice, but her focus hasn't wavered. While other lawyers chase every potential client like a dog chasing squirrels in the park, Sona's built a practice as focused as a laser beam.

The beautiful irony? By choosing to serve fewer people, she's actually built a more sustainable, successful practice. She's not just another estate planning lawyer, she's THE estate planning lawyer for young families in her community. It's like being the only pediatrician in a neighborhood full of new parents. You don't need every patient, you just need the right ones.

We are going to come back to her story later in the book in the chapter on marketing. Sona's story isn't just about finding a niche. It's about having the courage to stick to it. In a profession where FOMO (Fear Of Missing Out) can drive you to chase every potential client who fogs a mirror, Sona's dedication to her chosen niche is rarer than a quiet moment in a house full of toddlers.

Estate planning is usually a one-and-done business, like wedding photography but with more paperwork and less cake. Once you've helped a client plan their estate, they typically don't need you again for years. This makes Sona's success even more impressive. While my firm gets to nurture long-term relationships with our clients, estate planning attorneys need a constant stream of new faces walking through their doors.

This principle of knowing exactly what you do—and don't do—applies across all practice areas. Let me give you another example from a different field. Business law is complex enough without trying to be everything to everyone. Take my client who focuses exclusively on startup business law. When clients come to him with employment issues or personal injury cases, he doesn't hesitate; he refers them to specialists in those areas. Simple, clean, and effective.

This approach has made him the clear choice for startups in his market. No wavering, no "Maybe I could handle that employment contract." He knows his strength and sticks to it. He operates like any good specialist should. When something's outside his expertise, he has a network of trusted colleagues ready to help. The client gets the expert they need, the referral partner gets a well-matched client, and he maintains his reputation as someone who knows his boundaries and respects his niche.

It's not about rejecting business, it's about ensuring clients get the best possible service, even when that means directing them elsewhere. Being known as someone who puts clients' needs first builds more long-term success than trying to handle everything yourself.

The referral system works both ways. Other lawyers now consistently send him their startup cases, creating a reliable network of mutual support. He's built a sustainable practice by being clear about what he does—and doesn't—handle.

This level of focus isn't just good for his practice, it's good for his clients. They know exactly what they're getting: dedicated, specialized startup legal expertise without any distractions or divided attention.

One of my California clients has mastered the art of specialization, working exclusively with Hispanic business owners. Not just any business owners, but specifically

Hispanic entrepreneurs who need protection from lawsuits and employee disputes. In a state with tens of thousands of Hispanic-owned businesses, he's never short on clients.

His focus is laser-sharp, helping these business owners navigate California's complex legal landscape. No criminal law, no divorce cases, no real estate closings. Just pure business protection for a specific community that needs his expertise.

He understands his market's unique challenges, speaks their language (literally and figuratively), and has built a reputation as the go-to expert in his niche. When a Hispanic business owner in California faces legal troubles, his name comes up in conversations before any others.

His success demolishes the myth that you need to be all things to all people. He's proof that you can build a thriving practice by serving a specific community exceptionally well. No need for twenty different practice areas or a client base that looks like the United Nations.

Excellence attracts clients, not a menu of services. When you're the best at what you do, even in a narrow field, clients will seek you out. They're not looking for someone who's okay at everything; they want someone who's exceptional at solving their specific problems.

When it comes to billing...

Hourly billing is outdated, especially for small firms. The big firms can get away with it because their corporate clients aren't counting pennies when they're spending millions. But for firms serving small businesses? That meter running in the background creates more tension than a family dinner during election season.

We ditched hourly billing years ago after I got tired of having the same argument with clients: "You charged me $250 just to answer a question?" They'd see the bill but not the two hours of research behind that two-minute phone call. They couldn't see me reconciling trust accounts at midnight or strategizing tax savings over my morning coffee.

Now we create custom service packages based on what each client actually needs. It's not one-size-fits-all; some clients need more support than others. But every client knows exactly what they're paying for upfront.

The traditional law firm approach of 'bill, bill, bill, then write off half of it when the client complains' is exhausting for everyone involved. Your associates are pressured to hit billable targets, but the reality is stark: Lawyers typically bill only 2.9 hours of an eight-hour workday and then collect 90% of what they bill. In the end, you're only getting paid for about 30% of the time you are at work while creating stress for your team and suspicion from your clients.

Small business clients scrutinize every dollar, and they should. They're not massive corporations with bottomless legal budgets. When they get a bill full of six-minute increments, they're going to question everything. "Why did it take 0.3 hours to read my email?" "Did you really spend 1.2 hours on that phone call?" This adversarial billing relationship is one reason why, according to Clio's research, the average lawyer loses over a quarter of their billable work to write-offs and uncollected fees.

The industry is taking notice. While hourly billing remains the dominant model, firms are increasingly moving toward flat-fee structures. The 2024 Clio Legal Trends Report reveals that flat-fee billing amounts have grown by 34% since 2016, with a notable 6% jump in the past year alone. Smart firms are recognizing that predictable pricing creates better client relationships and more reliable cash flow.[5]

• •

The solution? Clear packages, clear communication. Your clients need to understand what they're getting. They need regular updates, progress reports, and the feeling that you're on their team, not just running a meter.

We learned this lesson the hard way in my practice. Clients don't see the backend work—the research, the planning, the double-checking. All they see is their interactions with us and the final product. That's why communication isn't just important, it's everything. Your brilliant legal work means nothing if your client doesn't understand its value.

Professional responsiveness shouldn't be a superpower, but in today's world, returning messages within 24 hours apparently makes you the Superman of client service. Our 24-hour response policy isn't rocket science, it's basic respect with a dash of common sense.

---

[5] 2024 Legal Trends Report," Clio Legal (January 2024).

The bar for professional communication is so low you could trip over it. Our clients constantly praise our "amazing responsiveness" simply because we do what should be standard: acknowledge their messages within a business day. Sometimes the response is just "Got your email, researching the answer, will get back to you by Wednesday." But guess what? That brief message prevents more anxiety for the client.

Want to know the number-one reason clients fire their current CPA or attorney? Radio silence. These professionals treat client communication like they're protecting nuclear launch codes. Weeks go by without a response, and suddenly their client is sitting in our office, telling horror stories about unanswered emails.

You don't need artificial intelligence or a team of communication ninjas to fix this. Just basic human decency and a calendar. Can't give a complete answer right away? Fine. But taking two weeks to say "I'm working on it" needn't be the case either.

Monthly flat fees aren't just about predictable billing. They're about transforming your relationship with clients from emergency responder to trusted advisor. At Counsel, we've structured our services like a premium streaming service, minus the annoying "Are you still watching?" prompts.

Here's how it works: Clients pay a set monthly fee that includes unlimited consultation and correspondence with our team. No more watching the clock during phone calls or hesitating to send that quick email. It's liberating, like an all-you-can-eat buffet of professional expertise.

Most clients don't need intensive support every single day. But when they *do* need it? They want someone who already knows their business inside and out. Not some random professional they found through a panicked Google search at 2 a.m.

The beauty of this system is its clarity. Everyone knows exactly what's included because it's all spelled out upfront. No surprises, no shock bills, no awkward conversations about six-minute increments. It's like having a prenup for your professional relationship; everything's clear from the start.

This approach transforms you from just another service provider into a genuine part of their team. We're not just the folks who prepare tax returns, we're an extension of their law firm. When they're making big decisions, we're already in the room (virtually or otherwise).

Structure these packages correctly, and everyone wins. Clients get the consistent support they need without financial anxiety. You get predictable revenue and deeper client relationships. Plus, you can focus on actually solving problems instead of documenting every minute of your day.

The monthly flat fee isn't just a pricing structure, it's a different way of practicing. Instead of being the professional equivalent of a fire department (only called in emergencies), you become more like a trusted family doctor who helps prevent problems before they start.

Structuring service packages for lawyers is trickier than for CPAs. Nobody wakes up and says, "I feel like filing some taxes today!" That's mandatory. But legal services? That's often seen as optional until there's a five-alarm emergency.

However, smart business owners want preventive legal care. They'd rather have a lawyer on speed dial than scramble to find one when things go sideways. That's where strategic package structuring comes in.

Start with the basics, the stuff businesses actually need. For a business law attorney, that means handling annual corporate filings, shareholder minutes, Statement of Information filings—the legal equivalent of oil changes and tire rotations. These are the maintenance items that every business needs, so why not be the firm that offers them?

Then add in the cherry on top: unlimited correspondence. Here's what makes this brilliant: business owners won't abuse it. They're not going to call you at midnight because they're bored. But when they *do* need you? You're there, already familiar with their business, ready to help.

Imagine a package where a $1,000 monthly retainer gets all their corporate maintenance plus the ability to reach out anytime. When a client calls saying, "I'm thinking about selling my business," you're included in that conversation from the start. Sure, the actual sale process would be additional—you're not giving away the farm here—but that initial strategy session is covered.

• •

This isn't about including everything under the sun. The goal is to create enough value that clients feel comfortable reaching out before small issues become legal disasters. It's like having a primary care physician—you might still need a specialist sometimes, but you've got someone watching your overall legal health.

The beauty of this model? Clients get peace of mind knowing they can pick up the phone without watching a billing clock tick away. You get a steady income and the chance to catch legal issues while they're still manageable. Everyone sleeps better at night, except maybe your competitors who are still billing in six-minute increments.

KEY TAKEAWAYS:

- **Own Your Niche:** Stop being a generalist. Pick a specific focus and become the go-to expert in that area.

- **Ditch Hourly Billing:** Create value-based service packages with monthly flat fees. Your clients want predictability, not surprises.

- **Systems First, Hiring Second:** Build clear processes before bringing on staff. You can't delegate what you haven't systematized.

- **Respond Within 24 Hours:** Quick response times aren't just good manners, they're good business. Clients will stay for communication alone.

- **Invest in Tomorrow:** Sometimes you need to earn less now to make more later. Strategic growth requires strategic investment.

CHAPTER 5

The Cash Catalyst: Igniting Your Profit Engine

When a new firm comes on board, we dive into their financials like detectives at a crime scene. Past tax returns and YTD financial statements are the starting point for understanding our clients' needs and goals. We want to see it all. And usually what we find is . . . interesting. Not always bad, but different. And by different, I sometimes mean, "Who taught you to categorize retainer deposit as income?" Here's the thing about profits: they come from working smarter, not just harder. Delegation isn't just about clearing your plate, it's about making room for higher-value work. But here's where many firms get stuck. They think everything needs to be done in-house, as if outsourcing is somehow cheating at business.

You don't need an in-house IT department any more than you need an in-house barista. That receptionist doing your bookkeeping? They might be lovely, but unless they moonlight as a CPA, that's probably not the best use of anyone's time. And don't get me started on firms that think they need a full marketing department down the hall.

For smaller firms, outsourcing non-core operations isn't just smart, it's survival. Why pay full-time salaries for part-time needs? Focus on what makes you money—practicing law. Everything else? There's probably someone who can do it better and cheaper than you can. But here's the real secret to profitability: You need to know your numbers. Not your "I think we're doing okay because the lights are still on" numbers, but real, solid Key Performance Indicators (KPIs). And you can't have reliable KPIs without reliable bookkeeping. It's like trying to lose weight with a broken scale—you're just guessing. Let's add a few examples of KPIs, such as profit margin, realization rate, utilization rate, collection rate, percentage of sales in marketing expenses, wages in relation to sales or case load, and in my opinion one of the most important KPIs for law firms, the average hourly rate (AHR) calculations. These are compared to your historic data but also with other firms in similar practice areas, geographic areas, and size.

AHR calculations are crucial KPI for measuring your firm's profitability per client or engagement. This is especially vital if you're doing flat fee billing, which is becoming more popular these days. But honestly, it matters just as much for traditional hourly billing because—let's face it—not all the hours your team works actually make it onto the invoice.

Here's how it works: You take the total fee you charged a client and divide it by the total hours your team spent on that engagement. This shows you what you're really making per hour.

For example, let's say you charge a client $10,000 for handling a matter, and it takes your firm 60 hours to complete everything. Your AHR would be $166 per hour. That sounds decent until you compare it with your costs. If you're paying your team an average of $100 per hour for this work, you're only making $66 per hour in profit. That's a 60% labor cost.

Between us, that's too high. In a healthy law firm, your labor costs should be around 30% of revenue, not 60%. You're leaving too much money on the table.

Now, you can measure AHR in different ways. The example I just gave includes everyone who touched the case, from receptionist to partner. You could also just track professional time (lawyers and paralegals) and exclude admin time, but then you'd need a higher AHR to compensate.

At my firm, we measure the time of everyone who works on an engagement to get the complete picture of profitability. I don't get caught up in who did what; what matters most is that the client is happy with our service, feels they got real value, and that we don't lose money. Does it really matter if my admin did more of the legwork than the lawyers? Or if we used AI to handle routine emails to make the project more efficient? Not at all. Results and profitability are what count.

Now, for flat fee billing firms specifically, remember that you're building long-term relationships, not just completing one-off transactions. There will be times when your AHR might be lower than you'd like, but if you're consistently delivering excellent service, you won't lose in the long run.

In my own practice, I can count on one hand how many clients we've lost in the 15 years I've been operating. This isn't because I've been nickel-and-diming them; quite the opposite. It's because I've maintained service quality regardless of the AHR for any particular engagement. That said, I have had several straightforward conversations with clients about increasing fees for future work when the numbers weren't adding up.

Here's a crucial point: With flat fee billing, you can't suddenly increase the fee mid-engagement because that would destroy trust. But I've found that nearly every time I've explained a fee increase for upcoming work, clients who were happy with our previous service stayed with us. That's what relationship-building is about, and in my opinion, it's the absolute best way to grow a firm. We'll revisit this concept later in the book when I share insights from my friend Sona A. Tatiyants.

Another advantage of tracking AHR for flat fee billing is that it helps identify opportunities to make your firm more efficient. Especially with the rise of AI, the possibilities for improving profitability while enhancing client service are practically limitless.

Talking about AI—yes, it's scary, but the truth is that it's here to stay. In 2023, Goldman Sachs published a study revealing that 44% of work tasks performed in the legal industry could be automated by AI, potentially replacing 40% of legal industry employees.[6]

Now, if you're charging flat fees and consistently delivering excellent service that keeps clients coming back, what does it matter to them whether you have a $120,000-a-year paralegal doing the work or if you're getting it done with AI, as long as quality control is maintained? Do you see the potential here? According to the 2024 Clio Legal Trends Report, "AI automation could reduce hourly billing per lawyer by $27,000 annually."[7]

If you think this isn't happening yet or is coming years from now, you're wrong. Per the same Clio report, 79% of lawyers have already adopted AI in some capacity, with 17% implementing wide adoption, 21% partial adoption, and 34% minimal adoption for now.

Do you think clients care if you use AI? Worried that if they know you're using AI, they won't like it? Wrong again. According to the 2024 Clio Legal Trends Report, nearly half of clients actually prefer to work with law firms that use AI, and 70% either prefer firms using AI or don't care if the firm uses it. This number is likely to increase in the near future, as it has already jumped from 46% in 2023.

The message is clear: Measure your AHR, find efficiencies where you can, and don't shy away from technologies that can help you deliver better service more profitably.

---

[6] Goldman Sachs. (2023, March 27). "The Potentially Large Effects of Artificial Intelligence on Economic Growth." Goldman Sachs Global Investment Research. Retrieved from https://www.gspublishing.com/content/research/en/reports/2023/03/27/d64e052b-0f6e-45d7-967b-d7be35fabd16.html.

[7] Clio Legal Trends Report, 2024.

••

Once you have accurate financial statements, the path forward becomes clearer than a lawyer's billable hour requirements. You can spot issues like paying $100,000 in rent when similar firms in your area pay $50,000. Sure, sometimes you're stuck with decisions like an expensive lease until it runs out, but at least you know where to focus your attention for the next round of improvements.

These insights are like planting seeds in our clients' minds. They might not sprout immediately, but when that lease renewal comes up, guess who's thinking twice about that premium downtown address? Remember, you can't improve what you can't measure, and you can't measure what you can't trust. Get your books in order first, then let the numbers guide your decisions.

A friend of mine offers a perfect example of how not to handle commercial real estate decisions. He's paying $7,500 monthly for a retail space that might as well be on Mars for all the foot traffic it gets. And what makes this even worse is that his business is entirely remote. His clients are scattered across the state, and exactly none of them care where his physical office sits.

So he's dropping $90,000 a year on a fancy address when he could run the same operation from a $3,000-a-month space tucked away in a less prestigious zip code. That's $54,000 in unnecessary expenses—enough to pay for a lot of help with things he does not want to do. It's like my firm paying for an advertisement in a medical association magazine. Sure, it's nice, but if I don't work with doctors and no lawyers will see it, what's the point? His clients care more about getting his attention and legal advice on time than admiring his gleaming office.

This is what happens when ego drives business decisions instead of economics. I hope he will skip this portion of the book when he reads it. A prestigious address means nothing if it's eating up your profits. For a firm with remote clients, paying premium rent is like buying a sports car to deliver pizza—impressive, but completely missing the point.

Software can make or break a modern law firm, yet I still see firms running their practice like it's 1985—all spreadsheets and sticky notes. It's like trying to compete in Formula 1 with a horse and buggy. We're Clio consultants, and no, this isn't a paid advertisement. But when you've seen enough law firms drowning in inefficiency, you get excited about solutions that actually work. Clio is essentially mission control for law firms, handling everything from client data to billing to time tracking, and actually much more than that now with Clio accounting, which is an accounting software directly within the practice management software (no this is not a threat to us since it is after all just software that makes everyone's job easier!) Think of it as the Swiss Army knife of legal practice management, minus the tiny scissors nobody knows how to use.

Clio is able to show you exactly who's pulling their weight and who's just pulling your leg. Do you want to know if your associates are billing 90% of their time or just looking busy while perfecting their coffee-making skills? Clio knows.

Just because you've moved to flat fee billing doesn't mean you can throw your time tracking out the window. Think of it this way: A restaurant with an all-you-can-eat buffet still needs to know how much food it is serving to stay profitable.

Even with flat fees, tracking time serves two crucial purposes. First, it lets you measure the actual profitability of each engagement. That client you thought was a great deal at $5,000? You might discover your team is spending twice as many hours as you budgeted, effectively halving your hourly rate. Without tracking time, you'd never know you were losing money.

Second, time tracking helps measure team efficiency. Each engagement should have a target budget of hours, even with flat fees. When someone consistently goes over budget, it might indicate they need additional training or that your processes need refinement. When they consistently come in under budget, you might have found a best practice worth replicating.

This data is invaluable for pricing future engagements too. Over time, you'll develop accurate estimates of how long different types of matters typically take, allowing you to set flat fees that are both competitive and profitable. You can't improve what you don't measure, and you can't set realistic flat fees if you don't know your true costs.

The goal isn't to nickel-and-dime clients like hourly billing does, but to ensure your flat fee structure is sustainable while delivering value to both your clients and your firm.

A lawyer working standard hours (2,080 annually) should be billing about 1,750-1,900 hours at 85-90% efficiency. At $350 per hour (being conservative here), that's $620,000-$650,000 in annual revenue per attorney. Not bad, right? But what happens when that same lawyer slacks off by just 10%? That tiny dip in productivity—with less than an hour of extra "research" (aka social media scrolling) per day—costs you $60,000-$65,000 annually. Per lawyer. Without proper tracking, that money disappears.

This isn't about turning your firm into a sweatshop with fancy software. It's about knowing your numbers so you can make informed decisions. Because if you can't measure it, you can't manage it. And if you can't manage it, you might as well be running your firm with a Magic 8-Ball. Without proper practice management software, you're flying blind and hoping really hard that everyone's doing what they should be.

The bottom line? Modern practice management tools aren't just fancy toys, they're oxygen for your firm's profitability. In today's legal market, the difference between success and struggle often comes down to how well you can track, measure, and optimize your firm's performance.

When we spot these efficiency slides, we don't storm into firms playing efficiency police. Instead, we arm managing partners with cold, hard data. It's amazing how differently a performance conversation goes when you can say, "This position needs 85-90% billable time, you're at 70%, and it's costing us exactly $109,200 a year," versus "You seem kind of slow lately."

But here's where most firms get it backward. They think bringing in more clients is the answer to everything, when in reality, adding clients to a broken system is like adding more cars to a traffic jam. It doesn't fix the problem, it just creates a bigger mess.

I learned this the hard way. Early in my practice, I thought like everyone else: "Two more clients and I can hire help! Then I'll have all the time in the world!" Spoiler alert: I got the clients, hired someone, and created chaos because I had no systems in place for my new hire to follow. The ingredients for my cook were there; I just didn't tell him what was on the menu and what needed to be served ASAP.

Your firm needs systems so clear that anyone can follow them. Think McDonald's—they're not serving better burgers than anyone else, but they've systematized everything so perfectly that they can turn anyone into a functional employee faster than any other establishment at the time of its opening.

The key is building your foundation before adding weight to the structure. Sure, more clients mean more revenue, but without proper systems, it's like trying to carry water in a leaky bucket—you're working harder but ending up just as empty.

Every business book preaches this, but we all think we're the exception. We're not. Growing revenue without fixing your foundation might solve the immediate problem, but it's not a long-term solution. The real growth strategy? Fix your systems first. Make them so clear that even a first-year associate couldn't mess them up (okay, maybe that's pushing it, but you get the point). Because when your processes are solid, growing your firm becomes about scaling success, not multiplying problems.

Most CPAs just crunch numbers and vanish until tax season, like groundhogs with calculators. We're building something different; we're the quarterbacks for our clients. They call us for everything. Need an insurance advisor? We know people. Making so much money you don't know what to do with it? (First, congratulations on this excellent problem.) We'll connect you with wealth advisors. But we don't just throw our clients over the fence to other professionals with a "good luck" wave. We stick around as translators and mediators. Because while our clients might be brilliant attorneys, some of them think diversification means having two different credit cards. And wealth advisors, bless their hearts, are often thinking about investments while ignoring little details like tax implications or that pesky thing called cash flow.

Take one of our clients from six years ago. When we found him, he had one employee, zero systems, and a bank account that echoed when you looked at it. He had practice management software (Clio), but he wasn't as effective as he could have been because he did not know how to maximize the benefit of Clio and he did not have time to learn it.

We dove in and started organizing everything from billing to case management. We didn't just show him how to use Clio; we actually ran it for him. Suddenly, bills were going out on time, collections were happening, and money started appearing in his account like magic (except it wasn't magic, it was just proper systems).

The real transformation? This lawyer suddenly had brain space to practice law instead of wondering why his billing was a mess or whether his employee would get paid this month. It's amazing how much better you can serve clients when you're not spending half your day wrestling with administrative chaos.

This isn't just about doing the work for them, though sometimes that's exactly what they need. It's about creating systems so clear that anyone could run them. Whether we handle it or train their team, the goal is the same: free up our clients to do what they do best—practice law and make money doing it.

Nobody goes to law school dreaming about invoicing clients or reconciling trust accounts. Just like I no longer get excited about tax returns. Sure, I'm good at them, but being good at something doesn't mean you have to spend your life doing it. That's like staying in a relationship just because you're really good at arguing.

I've shifted my time to what actually energizes me: strategic planning, client advising, and building relationships. The tax returns? They get done by my stellar team, with my eyes providing the final review. Many attorneys need this mentality shift more than they need another legal pad. They think if they don't personally touch every document, the legal world might implode.

Understanding your numbers and building the right systems is just the start. In the next chapter, we'll dive into how those numbers can expose the hidden money drains in your practice. From overpaying for services you don't need to undercharging for the ones you provide, we'll explore how to plug the financial leaks that are quietly draining your firm's profitability. Because knowing your numbers is important, but knowing what to do with them is what separates thriving firms from those just staying afloat.

Get ready to discover why some of your most "necessary" expenses might be completely unnecessary, and how small tweaks to your operations can lead to significant improvements in your bottom line. The difference between a profitable practice and a struggling one often comes down to knowing exactly where your money is going, and more importantly, where it shouldn't be.

KEY TAKEAWAYS:

- **Build Systems That Tell The Truth:** Your decisions are only as good as your data. Create systems that deliver reliable numbers, not guesswork.

- **Make Informed Mistakes:** When you have solid data, even mistakes become learning opportunities. Take calculated risks, not blind gambles.

- **Think Five Moves Ahead:** Plan multiple scenarios for your firm's future. Use your KPIs to guide strategic planning, not just track history.

- **Know Your Numbers Cold:** Monitor your Average Hourly Rate (AHR) religiously;it reveals what you actually earn, not just what you charge. Make this metric visible to all decision-makers, review it quarterly, and use the insights to guide your pricing and resource decisions. In the age of AI and automation, understanding your true profitability per engagement isn't just smart business, it's survival.

- **Act on Data, Not Hunches:** Trust your metrics over your gut. The most expensive decisions are the ones made without facts.

CHAPTER 6

Plugging the Leaks: How to Stop Hemorrhaging Money

Here's a story about missed opportunities and the power of having the right data. One of our clients came to us after years with another accounting firm. Their old routine? Dump a year's worth of financial statements on their CPA's desk each January, watch them get plugged into some software, and call it a day. It was about as strategic as using a weather app to predict last month's rainfall. Now, I'll admit that we used to operate this way too. Take the financials, crunch the numbers, and send an invoice. Rinse and repeat. But here's the problem: How can you give meaningful advice when you're looking at old financial data? By the time you spot a problem, it's ancient history.

I realized something important: When clients weren't getting strategic advice, it wasn't their fault. It was mine. They didn't know what was possible because I wasn't showing them. It's like having a Ferrari but only using it to drive to the grocery store. The potential was there, but nobody knew how to unlock it.

The same principle applies to law firm clients. They often don't know what they truly need until someone explains it to them. As trusted advisors, we have a responsibility that goes beyond just doing what clients ask. Sometimes what they request isn't actually what's best for them. It's our job to show them the full range of possibilities, to help them understand how different strategies might affect their decision-making, and to guide them toward solutions they might not even know exist. Simply taking orders isn't service, it's an abdication of our professional responsibility.

That's why we built our own in-house bookkeeping department. Now we won't take on clients unless we're handling their books. Sounds rigid? Maybe. But it's like a doctor insisting on running tests before prescribing medicine—you need accurate, current data to give good advice. The key was restructuring our service packages to show clients what's possible. Because clients don't care about debits and credits or which software we use. They care about value. They care about having someone who can tell them in October that they're on track to overpay their taxes by $50,000 if they don't make changes now, not someone who'll point this out in April when it's too late.

Let me share a perfect example of how real-time bookkeeping saved one of our law firm clients from a six-figure headache. This firm was growing fast, with the kind of growth that makes bankers smile and accountants nervous. By June, they were on track for their best year ever. The problem? Nobody was watching their estimated tax payments.

Without current books, they would have sailed right into December thinking everything was fantastic, only to discover they were underpaid on their quarterly estimates by about $120,000. Instead, because we were monitoring their books monthly, we caught this in July. We had time to adjust their remaining payments, set aside cash, and implement tax strategies before it was too late to prevent what could have been a devastating April 15th surprise.

Another client was hemorrhaging money on case costs for their contingency cases. Their old system? Throw receipts in a folder and deal with them at tax time. Real-time bookkeeping showed them they were spending in ways that were not captured in the accounting system to be applied toward cases. We caught this trend in their March numbers, helped them implement new cost control measures, and by year-end, they'd saved over $80,000 just by applying expenses to the cases they belonged to.

Here's my favorite: A three-partner firm was splitting profits equally, but real-time bookkeeping revealed one practice area was generating 70% of the firm's profit while eating only 30% of its resources. This data helped them restructure their partnership agreement to better reflect each partner's contribution, preventing what could have been a nasty partner dispute down the road.

These aren't just bookkeeping stories, they're profit preservation stories. When you can see the numbers as they happen, you can fix problems while they're still small. It's the difference between patching a small leak and dealing with a flooded basement.

Breaking Free from the Billable Hour

We dug into AHR billing in the last chapter. Let me share a few more details about how this works in our accounting practice, and why it works just as well for law firms.

In our firm, we bundle bookkeeping, consulting, tax planning, and preparation into comprehensive packages. When clients know they won't get a bill for asking a question, they actually ask questions. These questions often help us catch problems early, saving everyone time and money.

If your client is afraid to call because they know the clock is ticking at $400 an hour, they might sit on a small problem until it becomes a crisis.

Now, I know what you're thinking: *But Emil, this works for accounting.* Law is different. Is it, though? Yes, some practice areas like contingency-fee personal injury cases need different structures. But for many practice areas, package pricing is good business.

Take trust and estate work: Start with a flat fee for initial estate planning, then offer a small monthly retainer for ongoing advisory services with unlimited phone consultations. This gives clients peace of mind and you catch issues early.

Business attorneys can create similar value with monthly retainers covering routine advice and document reviews. Employment law attorneys might include monthly compliance reviews and regular handbook updates with their packages.

••

Let's talk practical implementation. In our firm, we operate on three service tiers. Each builds on the previous one, adding more value as the client's needs grow:

1. The base package includes essentials—your firm's "prevent disasters" level.

2. The middle tier is where most clients should land—your "sweet spot."

3. The premium tier is your "sleep like a baby" package with unlimited access and priority handling.

Transitioning existing hourly clients requires finesse. Start with your best clients; show them their last year's billings, then present a package that offers more value while costing slightly less. For skeptics, offer a trial period.

• •

Remember, this isn't about discounting, it's about right-sizing services for smaller clients.

The key is presenting packages as an upgrade in service, not just a billing change. And remember what we discussed about AHR—with flat fee billing, you can leverage efficiencies and technologies while still maintaining strong client relationships and predictable revenue.

According to the 2024 Clio Trend Report, flat fee billing has increased 20% since 2016, with firms collecting payments almost twice as fast as hourly billers and closing cases 2.6 times faster.

Let's be honest. If you provide enough value for an agreed fee, clients won't care about your profit margin. They've already agreed to the fee, and as long as you deliver what you promise, you've created a win-win situation.

Strategic Tax Planning That Actually Works

Most accountants treat client communication like they're using carrier pigeons—responses take weeks if they come at all. And when they do respond? It's usually just to say, "pay this" or "sign that." No strategy, no advice, just basic compliance work that a well-trained hamster could probably handle.

The entity structure your law firm chooses can absolutely make or break your growth trajectory.

This isn't just about paperwork and formalities. The wrong structure could cost you tens—sometimes hundreds—of thousands in overpaid taxes. That's money that should be fueling your firm's growth and helping you hire the right people, not padding the government's coffers.

Beyond the tax implications, the wrong structure can create significant internal problems between partners. For example, if multiple partners run their firm as a corporation, they'll be locked into more rigid arrangements under corporation law without the flexibility that partnership structures allow.

When I talk about partnerships, I'm referring to regular partnerships, Limited Liability Partnerships (LLPs), and Limited Liability Companies (LLCs). The right choice often depends on your state's regulations. California, for instance, doesn't allow law firms to operate as LLCs; firms there typically use LLP structures to get the partnership advantages. Other states, like Texas or Ohio, permit professional LLCs, which offer similar benefits.

One major advantage of partnership structures is how profits can be allocated. As long as partners agree, practically anything can be outlined in the partnership agreement. No, not literally anything, but you get my point.

Both LLPs and LLCs provide the flexibility I'm talking about while also offering liability protection that a general partnership doesn't provide. See what I'm getting at? They're all partnerships offering flexibility, but only LLPs and LLCs shield you from certain liabilities.

From the client's perspective, these distinctions likely won't matter. But for you and your partners? The difference could determine whether your firm thrives or merely survives.

• •

Business owners want someone who can do more than just calculate their tax bill. They're craving actual guidance, real strategies, proactively and not retroactively. They're busy enough trying to keep up with case law; they shouldn't have to become tax experts too. That's where we come in, doing more than just pushing papers and crunching numbers. We're talking operational support, the kind that keeps your back office running smoother than a Tesla on autopilot. But it's not just about keeping the lights on, it's about strategic tax planning that puts more money in your pocket.

Take retirement planning, for instance. Most lawyers are so busy building their practice they forget to build their future. Or consider this gem: putting your kids on payroll. I've got my 11-year-old shredding documents and collecting mail. Pay each kid a reasonable salary and you're looking at tax savings that matters. That's not creative accounting, that's smart business.

Building Generational Wealth

Maybe you thought I was kidding, but when I started putting my kids on payroll, I realized I had a bigger opportunity than just tax savings. This was my chance to teach financial education that most people don't learn until they're drowning in credit card debt. We set up a simple but powerful system. Every time my kids get paid (yes, for actual work; the IRS isn't known for their sense of humor), their money gets split three ways. Think of it as the world's smallest diversification strategy: savings, spending, and investing.

The savings portion is non-negotiable; it's their "sleep well at night" fund. My 11-year-old probably doesn't need an emergency fund yet, unless there's a critical Lego shortage on the horizon, but as James Clear explains in *Atomic Habits,* it's these small, consistent behaviors that compound into life-changing results. Clear would recognize this as a perfect example of habit stacking—linking the receipt of money directly to the act of saving, making the behavior automatic rather than optional.

This teaches them that you pay yourself first, before the money mysteriously evaporates into video game purchases. The spending portion is their "freedom fund." They can blow it on whatever they want (within reason—no underground bunkers or pet tigers). But here's the catch: once it's gone, it's gone. No advances on next month's pay, no dipping into savings. Clear would argue that this immediate feedback loop—watching your Roblox account hit zero with two weeks left in the month—is exactly the kind of clear consequence that helps cement good habits. It's not about the amount saved. It's about building the neural pathways that make saving as automatic as breathing.

What looks like a simple allowance system is actually creating what Clear calls an "identity-based habit." These kids aren't just learning to save money, they're becoming people who understand financial responsibility. The compound effect of these small financial decisions, made consistently over time, will shape their entire relationship with money.

The investment portion is where things get interesting. We sit down together and look at companies they understand. When my son wanted to buy Disney stock, we talked about why people buy Disney products and services. Now he watches their quarterly earnings with more interest than she watches their movies (maybe not exactly but close enough).

But the real magic happens in the conversations. When my kids want to buy something, we talk about opportunity cost. When they earn interest, we discuss compound growth.

When they make a bad spending decision (and they will), we talk about buyer's remorse. These aren't lectures, they're real-world lessons with real money. The goal isn't to raise mini-Warren Buffetts (though I wouldn't complain). It's about teaching them that money is a tool, not a mystery. By the time they're adults, they'll have over a decade of practical experience managing money. That's worth more than any tax savings.

The relationship between real estate and the tax code is like a carefully choreographed dance, where knowing the steps can save you thousands. But just owning property isn't enough. You need to understand how to leverage it properly within your overall financial strategy. Let's break down how the tax code really works with real estate. When you buy a residential rental property, you're not just investing in real estate, you're opening up a treasure chest of tax benefits. You can depreciate the building (not the land) over 27.5 years, deduct mortgage interest, property taxes, insurance, repairs, and yes, even that landscaper who charges more than your first hourly rate as a lawyer.

But here's where it gets really interesting: the long game. When properly structured, real estate can become a generational wealth transfer tool. Your heirs can inherit property at what's called a "stepped-up basis," meaning if you bought a property for $300,000 that's worth $1 million when you die, your heirs' new basis is $1 million. That's $700,000 of appreciation that completely escapes capital gains tax. Try getting that kind of tax treatment from your stock portfolio. For law firm owners looking to supercharge their retirement savings while creating current tax deductions, Cash Balance Plans are the secret weapon most people miss. Unlike a traditional 401(k) that caps out at $23,500 (plus catch-up contributions if you're over 50this is the tax year 2025 limit), a Cash Balance Plan can allow you to contribute significantly more—sometimes several hundred thousand dollars annually, depending on your age and income level. I usually call the Cash Balance Plan "401(k) on steroids."

Think about it: you're not just saving for retirement, you're creating massive current-year tax deductions and reinvesting the money you saved from the tax planning to let it grow for your retirement instead of paying Uncle Sam. A properly structured Cash Balance Plan, combined with a 401(k), can reduce your taxable income substantially. I've seen law firm partners cut their tax bills by six figures using this strategy alone. But here's the catch, and it's a big one: None of these strategies work in isolation. You need regular communication with your tax advisor. I'm talking quarterly at minimum, not just an annual tax-season scramble. Your CPA should be as familiar with your financial goals as they are with their own coffee order.

For those looking to start optimizing their tax strategy immediately, here are some concrete steps:

Start with vehicle deductions, but do it right. That means detailed mileage logs or actual expenses, not rough estimates that make IRS auditors raise their eyebrows. Use an app to track everything; technology is your friend here.

Time your equipment purchases strategically. Section 179 expensing and bonus depreciation can create significant tax savings, but timing matters. Sometimes pushing a purchase into January versus December (or vice versa) can make a huge difference in your tax picture, depending on current year vs. future years' projected income, tax bracket, and constant changes in the tax law.

Get smart about charitable giving. Consider donor-advised funds to bunch multiple years of charitable contributions into one year for maximum tax impact. It's not just about being generous, it's about being strategically generous. Implement a health savings account (HSA). This often-overlooked tool can turn personal medical expenses into business deductions while providing a valuable benefit to you and your employees. We can also write about structured settlements for contingency case law firms that make a big settlement in a year and might not make as much for a couple of years thereafter. Investments leveraged with loans for tax planning purposes is another very lucrative vehicle to help with tax planning, which can typically get five to ten times the deduction of the investment amount.

Smarter Planning

The Pass-Through Entity Tax Deduction (PTE Deduction) is a strategy that is particularly powerful for law firms. This is a game-changer for all pass-through entities including S-Corporations, LLCs, LLPs, and Partnerships, which cover most law firms.

Here's what makes this so powerful: It allows partners to pay a portion of their individual state income taxes directly from the business and get a deduction for it. These are taxes you'd have to pay anyway with personal funds, but with proper planning, you can pay them through your firm and save tens of thousands of dollars.

This example still makes me shake my head. We recently signed a law firm with two partners generating close to $2 million in annual profit. Their previous CPA never told them about this strategy, which turned out to be an extremely costly oversight.

These partners practice in California. With $2 million in profit, they could have paid $186,000 in personal state taxes through their law firm, which would have saved them over $70,000 per year. This tax code took effect in 2021, so they missed out on approximately $300,000 in tax savings over four years, just because nobody planned ahead with a strategy that takes only a couple of hours to implement.

Unfortunately, this isn't a strategy that allows us to amend previous years' returns to recoup those lost savings. The good news is we can implement it going forward and capture the benefits as long as the tax code remains in effect. And there are other tax planning tools that do allow us to go back and amend up to three years of returns to get refunds for clients whose previous advisors dropped the ball.

This is just one example of how devastating poor tax planning can be to a firm's growth. When you leave money like this on the table, you're not just paying more taxes, you're sacrificing capital that could be reinvested in your firm's future.

These tax strategies we've explored can significantly impact your firm's profitability. But there's another area where attention to detail and proper structures are equally critical, perhaps even more so since your license could be on the line.

That brings us to our next chapter on Trust Accounting. If you think the IRS is particular about documenting deductions, wait until you see how state bars handle trust accounts. We'll dive into the pitfalls that can sink even experienced attorneys (spoiler alert: commingling funds is just the tip of the iceberg), and the best practices that will help you sleep at night instead of worrying about random audits.

Because at the end of the day, trust accounting isn't just about compliance, it's about protecting your practice and your license. From setting up the right systems to avoiding common mistakes that make bar counsel's eyes twitch, we'll cover everything you need to know about managing client funds without losing your mind (or your license). Because keeping your profits is about protecting yourself from the kinds of mistakes that can cost you everything you've built. And trust accounting errors top that list of preventable disasters.

KEY TAKEAWAYS:

- **Real-Time Financial Clarity:** Monitor your numbers as they happen, not months later. You can't fix problems you can't see, and you can't seize opportunities you don't know exist.

- **Package Your Services Strategically:** Move beyond hourly billing to create predictable revenue and better client relationships. Structure service packages that encourage clients to seek help before small issues become expensive problems.

- **Build Smart Tax Strategies:** From employing family members to leveraging real estate, understand and implement tax strategies that build long-term wealth, not just short-term savings.

- **Think Beyond Today:** Whether it's teaching financial literacy to the next generation or structuring charitable giving, focus on strategies that create lasting value, not just immediate tax benefits.

- **Document Everything:** From tax deductions to charitable giving, proper documentation isn't just good practice, it's essential protection. This sets up the next chapter's focus on trust accounting.

CHAPTER 7

Law Firm Trust Accounting: Pitfalls & Best Practices

Here is a masterclass in how *not* to handle client funds, with Tom Girardi as the subject in question. Girardi makes Bernie Madoff look like an amateur when it comes to mishandling other people's money. This isn't just another cautionary tale about trust accounting. It's a Hollywood thriller complete with stolen millions, reality TV stars, and enough ethical violations to make your law school ethics professor need smelling salts.

Girardi wasn't just any lawyer, he was the king of plaintiffs' litigation in California and the guy who inspired the movie *Erin Brockovich*. The attorney who could charm juries and judges alike. But behind that polished exterior? He was running what amounted to a Ponzi scheme with his clients' settlement funds.

A Trail of Broken Lives

One of the most gut-wrenching examples involves Joe Ruigomez, whose story was featured on Netflix's *The Housewife and the Hustler.* In 2010, Joe survived a horrific gas explosion that killed his girlfriend and left him with devastating burns requiring countless surgeries. Girardi won him a substantial settlement, then proceeded to do his best disappearing act with the money. While Joe was struggling to pay for his medical care, Girardi was funding his wife Erika Jayne's pop music career and their obscenely lavish lifestyle.

Where was the California State Bar in this? Despite receiving complaint after complaint about Girardi's misconduct, they did nothing. Why? Probably because Girardi had spent decades cultivating relationships with bar officials, judges, and anyone else who might pose a threat to his scheme.

Fast forward to 2023, and the house of cards finally collapsed. Girardi, 85 and claiming dementia (convenient timing, no?), is still, as of the writing of this book, awaiting sentencing after being convicted of wire fraud and ordered to pay millions of dollars in restitution. His much younger wife, Erika Jayne of *Real Housewives of Beverly Hills* fame, filed for divorce faster than you can say "forensic accounting." The really horrifying part? This wasn't just a few million here and there. We're talking hundreds of millions of dollars stolen from clients, many of them victims of serious injuries, plane crashes, and other tragedies. While Girardi and his wife were flying private jets and living in a $13 million mansion, his clients were struggling to pay medical bills with settlement money they never received.

The Lion Air Flight 610 disaster unfolded on October 29, 2018, when a Boeing 737 MAX plunged into the Java Sea thirteen minutes after takeoff from Jakarta. All 189 passengers and crew perished. The crash investigation revealed critical failures in Boeing's MCAS system, a tragic story of corporate negligence that should have ended with grieving families receiving some measure of justice. Instead, they became victims twice over, thanks to Tom Girardi. Each family was promised $2 million in settlements, a number that could never make up for their losses but might at least provide some financial security. Girardi, acting as their champion in court, secured these settlements. Then he proceeded to help himself to at least $7.5 million of their money, while families waited for funds that would never arrive because Girardi was busy funding his wife's pop music career, private jet travel, and a lifestyle that made The Great Gatsby look restrained.

But the Lion Air families weren't alone. In Hinkley, California—the town made famous by activist and campaigner Erin Brockovich—residents who'd already suffered through groundwater contamination got victimized again when Girardi skimmed millions from their settlements. He did the same to victims of a blood-thinner drug that caused internal bleeding, another group of Indonesian airplane crash victims, and former NFL players suffering from brain injuries. Even children with cancer weren't spared from his greed.

The Price of Justice Delayed

When justice finally caught up with him in 2023, the charges read like a speedrun of the criminal code: five counts of wire fraud, massive client theft, running a Ponzi scheme with settlement funds, and tax evasion, because apparently, stealing from clients wasn't enough.

During his trial, Girardi pulled his final disappearing act, claiming dementia and hearing problems prevented him from attending in person. Meanwhile, his victims testified about losing homes and going bankrupt while waiting for money he'd already spent on his wife's designer clothes and their $13 million mansion.

Prosecutors laid bare his scheme: fake client costs, double-billing, lying about settlements, and shuffling money between accounts like a three-card monte dealer. He used new settlement money to pay old clients, running a Ponzi scheme that would have made Charles Ponzi himself blush.

Girardi's fall from grace took others down with him. His son-in-law was disbarred, former employees face charges, and the California State Bar is undergoing reforms that suggest someone finally found their spine after decades of looking the other way.

The point of this story? I want to introduce you to someone who knows more about keeping lawyers out of trouble than anyone else I know. Erin Joyce and I have crossed paths many times over the years, and I can tell you, if your law firm needs guidance on ethics and compliance in California, she's who you want in your corner.

Before she started helping attorneys stay on the right side of it, Erin spent nearly twenty years on the other side of the table as a prosecutor for the State Bar of California. Think about that; she's seen every mistake a lawyer can make, from both sides of the courtroom. She's tried dozens of state bar cases and handled countless appeals. When it comes to understanding how state bar investigations unfold, she's quite literally written the book. But Erin's experience goes beyond just state bar proceedings. She started her career in intellectual property law, then took a fascinating detour as Chief Special Investigator for the Los Angeles Fire Department before joining the Office of Chief Trial Counsel. Now in private practice, she helps firms navigate the complex waters of professional responsibility and ethics.

I've watched Erin help numerous firms implement proper compliance systems, and let me tell you, having her perspective is like having a former IRS agent as your advisor in a tax audit. She knows exactly what regulators look for because she used to be one. When we sat down to discuss trust accounting and ethical compliance, her insights were so valuable I knew I had to share them with you.

The New Client Trust Account Protection Program and State Bar Changes

When Erin and I discussed the changing landscape of trust accounting in California, her first warning was clear: Change is coming, and it's coming fast. "We're looking into the third year for the implementation of the client trust account protection program," she explained. "The state bar has hired forensic accountants in the last 18 months to conduct random audits of client trust accounts that will be implemented soon. What's interesting is that the audit function isn't housed within the Office of Chief Trial Counsel, it's in the Office of Attorney Regulation."

This matters because the Office of Attorney Regulation is expanding its role beyond just basic member services. They're not just handling address changes anymore, they're conducting serious audits. Recently, they've started cross-referencing attorney state bar profiles with financial institution reports to ensure all trust accounts are properly registered.

"Every lawyer that maintains a trust account has to have it reported on their State Bar profile," Erin emphasizes. "So many lawyers just didn't understand that."

The state bar even tried something novel—it invited firms to volunteer for audits. "They sent out an email saying, 'Hey, who wants to be a guinea pig?'" Erin recalls with a laugh, "Any client of mine that asked, I said, 'No, don't do it.' I don't think it would lead to discipline, per se. But who wants to purposely open up your records if you don't have to?"

The challenge, Erin explains, lies in balancing compliance with client confidentiality. While Rule 1.15 requires lawyers to comply with state bar audit requests, there are still questions about how broad these audits can be. Traditionally, if a trust account check bounces, that gives the state bar probable cause to investigate that specific transaction. But what about everything else in those records?

"My experience is, everything in those records not related to that particular transaction is always redacted," Erin says. "But these audits won't be like that. They're going to ask for records for all these non-complaining clients, no waivers. We don't know how that's going to go yet."

The push for random audits isn't new; the state bar has wanted this authority for years. But it took the Girardi scandal to finally make it happen. "They've been wanting to do random audits, just like they started in 2011 to do random audits of MCLE compliance," Erin explains. "But it wasn't until the Girardi situation that they had the political cover to get the approval."

Common Trust Accounting Mistakes and Misconceptions

In my years of handling trust accounting for law firms, I've noticed a fundamental misunderstanding of what proper trust accounting actually requires. When I sat down with trust accounting expert Erin Joyce, she confirmed what I've been seeing in practice after practice.

Most lawyers, especially in personal injury, think they're doing everything right. They carefully handle each settlement, creating distribution sheets, calculating attorney fees, reducing medical bills, and getting client signatures. While this careful case-by-case tracking is essential, it's not actually trust accounting.

As Erin confirmed in our discussion, this process, while important, doesn't satisfy the requirements of Rule 1.15. The key difference—and I see this confusion with new clients constantly—is that true trust accounting requires maintaining a running balance that shows exactly how much belongs to each client at any moment. You need to track every transaction in real-time and be able to generate detailed reports instantly.

When law firms come to us, they often think they're complying because they keep meticulous records of individual transactions. But as Erin noted in our conversation, and as I've been teaching clients for years, proper trust accounting goes far beyond that. You need specialized accounting software that prevents you from writing checks when funds aren't available, even if the overall account balance could cover it.

Another common issue I see, which Erin also highlights, is lawyers jumping the gun on deposits. Yes, clients want their money quickly. Yes, your banker might give you instant credit because of your relationship. But if that check bounces a week later, you're looking at a cascade of insufficient funds problems that could trigger a state bar audit.

Even simple things like check management can create major problems. Erin shares a story about lawyers mixing up operating and trust account checks because they kept them together. This matches what we've seen in our practice— seemingly small oversights that create big headaches.

As Erin grimly notes, "The state bar teaches by discipline."

But it doesn't have to be that way. With proper systems and support, these issues are entirely preventable. That's why we insist on handling trust accounting comprehensively for our clients—because one small mistake can have devastating consequences.

One of the most dangerous misconceptions I hear regularly from lawyers is about excess funds in IOLTA accounts. "I'm not worried about my trust account," they'll tell me, "because I know I have more money in there than what I owe my clients." They think having extra money is playing it safe.

This couldn't be more wrong. In fact, it's a serious violation of state bar regulations. Erin and I both agree that any amount exceeding $500 over what you owe your clients is considered mishandling your trust accounting. This isn't just about having enough money to cover your obligations, it's about knowing exactly how much belongs to each client, down to the penny.

This is why proper reconciliation is so critical. It's not enough to know you have "more than enough" money in the account. You need to know precisely how much belongs to whom at any given moment. When lawyers tell me they're "sure" they have sufficient funds without being able to show exact balances, that's usually a red flag that their trust accounting needs immediate attention.

The state bar doesn't want to see extra money in your trust account any more than it wants to see too little. That's why we insist on reconciling our clients' IOLTA accounts to the penny on a regular basis, because being off by a thousand dollars too much can be just as problematic as being off by a thousand too little.

Three-way Reconciliation Requirements

Three-way reconciliation is one of the most crucial aspects of trust accounting, yet it's often the most misunderstood. When law firms handle their own reconciliations, I often see them missing critical steps in the process. Erin confirms the issues we encounter daily with our clients.

Every month, we perform detailed reconciliations comparing bank statements, accounting software, and client ledgers. It's not enough to just check that the numbers match; you need to understand and document every discrepancy. As Erin noted in our discussion, there are usually "explainable differences," like outstanding checks that haven't cleared yet. But these need to be tracked and resolved, not just noted.

One of the biggest mistakes I see firms make is thinking their responsibility ends when they write a check. In fact, that's just the beginning. We regularly encounter situations where small settlement checks go uncashed because the recipient thinks it's not worth the trouble. But as Erin confirms, you can't just let these funds sit in your trust account indefinitely.

Our process includes aggressive follow-up on outstanding checks. If a check is still outstanding after the first month, that's normal. But by month three, you need to take action: tracking down recipients, confirming addresses, and potentially stopping and reissuing payments. This level of diligence is what keeps firms compliant.

Perhaps the most dangerous misconception I encounter—and one that Erin strongly warns against—is firms thinking extra money in their trust account is a good thing. Let me be absolutely clear: Having unidentified funds in your trust account is a serious violation. When you certify compliance with the state bar, you're stating under penalty of perjury that you know exactly whose money is in that account. As Erin emphasizes, false certification can lead to suspension of your license.

This is why we insist on handling every aspect of trust accounting for our clients. The stakes are simply too high to risk any mistakes in this area.

Handling Historical Reconciliation Issues

One of the most daunting challenges we face is helping firms clean up years of unreconciled trust accounts. When meeting with trust accounting expert Erin Joyce, I wanted to confirm our approach to these sensitive situations.

Under Rule of Professional Conduct 1.15, firms must maintain deposit records for five years from the last disbursement. As Erin notes, and as we regularly advise our clients, state bar audits can reach back five years, while banks maintain records for seven. This aligns perfectly with our forensic accounting process for new clients.

To properly reconstruct trust records, we need complete

documentation: all bank statements, deposit records, incoming wire transfers, and every check written from the account. Each transaction must be tied to a specific client or case. Some firms still try to maintain these records in written ledgers, but as Erin emphasizes, that's no longer considered competent practice. Modern trust accounting requires technological solutions—something we've been telling clients for years.

When we encounter mysterious balances during reconstruction, we apply a simple test that Erin confirms: Is it third-party money or not? In our experience handling these situations, legitimate claims to trust funds rarely go unclaimed for years. As Erin points out, vendors like chiropractors or collection agencies don't quietly wait five years for payment.

This kind of deep forensic work often reveals a broader issue I see constantly in law firms, and one that Erin highlighted in our discussion. Most lawyers are so focused on practicing law that administrative duties take a back seat. But here's the irony: It's rarely their legal expertise that gets them in trouble with the state bar. It's these back-office functions, especially trust accounting, that pose the greatest risk to their license.

This is exactly why we insist on handling all aspects of trust accounting for our clients. When your license to practice law hangs in the balance, these administrative functions aren't just bookkeeping, they're professional life insurance.

Trust Accounting 101:
The Basics of Survival

I've seen one truth repeatedly confirmed: Nothing ends a legal career faster than trust accounting mistakes. The consequences aren't just financial, they're terminal for your practice. When we sat down with trust accounting expert and ethics attorney Erin Joyce, she reinforced everything we've been teaching our clients about the critical nature of proper trust management.

• •

Let me be absolutely clear about the fundamental rule: Settlement money isn't yours until you've earned it. That check might have your firm's name on it, but it belongs in a trust account, not your operating account. We've seen too many firms blur this line, and the results are never good.

There's an old saying in our office: "If you're not going to keep score, don't play the game." This isn't just clever phrasing, it's the philosophy that drives our entire approach to trust accounting. Every client's funds must be tracked to the penny, with immaculate records and regular three-way reconciliations.

Many firms come to us confused about what a three-way reconciliation actually entails. It's a precise matching between your bank statement, accounting software, and case management system. All three must align perfectly. In our practice, we perform these reconciliations monthly for our clients, ensuring nothing falls through the cracks.

California's move toward random audits has raised the stakes even higher. As we've been warning our clients, and as Erin confirmed in our discussion, other states are likely to follow California's lead. The scariest cases we see are firms that don't realize they're in trouble until they're facing serious consequences. One small mistake in trust accounting can cascade into a career-ending disaster.

That's why we've developed rigorous systems to protect our clients from these risks. When you're dealing with trust accounts, there's no such thing as a small error, only disasters waiting to happen.

Building a Bulletproof Trust Accounting System

Setting up proper trust accounting systems starts with the fundamentals. You need three distinct components: a dedicated trust bank account, robust accounting software that handles trust accounting, and a solid case management system. And no, your Excel spreadsheet from 2015 doesn't count as any of these.

Your trust account needs to be completely separate from your operating account—not just a different account number, but a different universe entirely. Many banks offer specific IOLTA accounts designed for law firms. Get one. Make sure it's properly designated and that the bank understands it's a trust account. This isn't just about organization, it's about ensuring the bank handles the account correctly and that any interest goes where it's supposed to.

Your accounting software should be designed for law firms. QuickBooks is fine for many things, but for trust accounting, you need something that understands legal trust accounting rules. The software needs to automatically maintain individual client ledgers, prevent overdrafts, and generate those three-way reconciliation reports that keep bar auditors happy.

This is where modern practice management software becomes crucial. Platforms like Clio, Smokeball, MyCase, and Filevine don't just manage your cases, they integrate seamlessly with your accounting software to create a complete financial management system. When your practice management software talks directly to QuickBooks or other accounting platforms, you eliminate manual data entry, reduce errors, and create an automatic audit trail. Plus, these integrations make three-way reconciliation much simpler because all your systems are automatically synced and updated in real-time.

• •

Now, for the pitfalls that can end your career. The biggest one? Commingling funds. This happens when lawyers treat their trust account like a convenience store cash register, mixing client funds with firm money. Even accidentally depositing a fee check into the trust account can trigger this violation.

Another common disaster: floating funds. This is when you distribute money from one client's settlement using another client's funds because the first settlement hasn't cleared yet. It might seem harmless; the money's coming, right? Wrong. This is the kind of thinking that gets lawyers introduced to the disciplinary committee.

Then there's the "borrowing" trap. A lawyer needs quick cash for office expenses and figures they'll just "borrow" from the trust account and replace it next week. Spoiler alert: This ends badly. Always. It doesn't matter if you replace it in an hour; once you've dipped into trust funds, you've crossed a line that can't be uncrossed.

Documentation failures are another killer. Every single transaction needs a paper trail clearer than a desert highway. Missing a deposit slip or failing to note which client a withdrawal belongs to isn't just sloppy, it's potentially career-ending.

Your system absolutely must include individual client ledgers tracking every penny in and out, regular monthly reconciliations, clear documentation for every transaction, and separation of duties where one person handles money and another does reconciliation. You need written policies and procedures, regular staff training, and automated alerts for low balances or unusual activity.

KEY TAKEAWAYS:

- **Trust Accounting Is Non-Negotiable:** Proper trust account management isn't just good practice, it's essential for keeping your license. One mistake can end a career, regardless of intent.

- **Systems Before Scale:** Establish proper trust accounting systems before growing your practice. Your processes must be bulletproof before you increase volume.

- **Three-Way Reconciliation Is Your Friend:** Regular three-way reconciliation between your bank statement, accounting software, and case management system isn't optional, it's your early warning system for problems.

- **Never "Borrow" From Trust:** No circumstance justifies dipping into trust funds, even temporarily. The moment you touch trust money inappropriately is the moment you cross a line you can't uncross.

- **Document Everything:** If it's not documented, it didn't happen. Keep meticulous records of every trust transaction. Your license may depend on it.

- **Excess funds in your trust account is not OK.**

CHAPTER 8

Magnetic Appeal

Earlier in this book, we met Sona A. Tatiyants, the estate planning attorney who built a thriving practice by focusing exclusively on young families. Her story isn't just about finding a niche. It's a masterclass in marketing and brand building without spending a dime on traditional advertising.

When you think about marketing a law firm, your mind might jump to billboards, radio spots, or social media campaigns. But Sona's approach proves there's a more effective way to build a practice. By creating genuine connections and understanding exactly whom she wanted to serve, she developed a marketing strategy that feels more like community building than promotion.

Her methods aren't just for estate planning attorneys; they can work for any practice area. Whether you're a business lawyer, family law practitioner, or litigation specialist, the principles she used to build her firm from scratch offer a blueprint for sustainable growth through strategic relationship building.

Let's dive into how she did it, and more importantly, how
you can apply these same principles to your practice. Sona's
story started in an unexpected place—law school. "I did not
want to go to law school," she admits with a laugh. "I wanted
to go to UCLA to become a writer. But my best friend was
applying to law school, and my mom suggested I try too. He
hated it, and I stuck it out."

What drew her to estate planning wasn't the technical
aspects, it was the human element. She took a class from a
practicing attorney who taught through stories about real
clients and relationships. "I tried various different things in
law school," Sona explains. "I clerked for a judge, worked
for an insurance defense firm, worked for nonprofits. What
I really homed in on is that I like working with people. I like
representing individuals who can talk to me and say 'You
really helped me,' versus saving $300,000 for an insurance
company."

This people-first approach would become the foundation
of her marketing strategy. When she launched her firm, everyone told her focusing on young families was financial suicide.
"These people have no money; you're going to go bankrupt,"
they warned. But Sona saw something others missed: "I have
a house, I'm married, and I'm having a child, and I think it's
important for me to plan."

She set out to build the kind of firm where she would
want to work—one that understood the needs of young
families.

Building From Zero

Before we get back to Sona's story, let me share something about intentionality that took me years to learn. When I first started my practice, I tried to be everything to everyone. Restaurants, tech startups, medical practices—if they needed accounting help, I was their guy. I thought casting a wide net would bring in more business. Instead, it brought more headaches.

Every new client meant learning a whole new industry, new regulations, new challenges. My team was constantly switching gears, trying to master different software systems and compliance requirements. One day we'd be figuring out tip reporting for a restaurant, the next we'd be dealing with venture capital accounting for a startup. It wasn't just inefficient, it was exhausting.

The frustration wasn't just on our end. Clients could tell we were stretching ourselves thin. They needed an expert in their industry, and instead they got someone who was adequate at everything but exceptional at nothing. It's like going to a doctor who treats humans, dogs, and houseplants. Sure, they might know the basics, but do you really want them performing your surgery?

The turning point came when I started focusing exclusively on law firms. Suddenly, everything got clearer. When a new prospect calls now, I often know their problems before they finish explaining them. Not because I'm psychic, but because I've seen the same patterns hundreds of times. Law firm accounting has specific pain points, and after working with nothing but law firms, these patterns become obvious.

This specialization changed everything. My team became more confident because they were dealing with the same types of challenges repeatedly. Our processes became more streamlined because we weren't constantly adapting them for different industries. Most importantly, we started providing more value to our clients because we weren't just solving their current problems; we could anticipate and prevent future ones.

Now when a law firm calls, I don't have to sell our services. Instead, I can say, "Let me guess; you're struggling with trust accounting compliance, your billing is running behind, you're not sure if your practice is as profitable as it should be, and your current CPA is not sitting down with you to advise and help you reduce your tax liability." The relief in their voice is immediate. They know they're talking to someone who understands their world.

Being intentional about your niche doesn't just make your work easier, it transforms how clients see you. You're no longer just a service provider, you're a specialist who intimately understands their challenges. It's the difference between being a general contractor and being the person who only restores historic homes. One is hired because they're available; the other is hired because they're irreplaceable.

This same principle of intentionality extends beyond just choosing your niche. It affects how you structure your firm, how you train your team, how you market your services— everything. When you're intentional about every aspect of your practice, decisions become clearer because you have a defined framework for making them.

• •

"I started with literally zero clients," Sona tells me over coffee in a diner in Glendale. "I sent out a letter to everyone I knew—law school classmates, previous colleagues, everyone—saying I was starting a firm. From that, I actually got a couple clients. My mom's friend became a client, and another woman from my mommy & me class became a client."

But here's where Sona's approach gets interesting. Instead of casting a wide net, she became intensely focused on building the right kind of practice. "I was very intentional," she emphasizes. "I set out to create a place where people could bring their kids, where we could have toys, where I could talk to a nursing mother—things you would never think would happen in a law firm."

Her networking strategy was equally methodical. In those early days, she scheduled her limited childcare time strategically: "I had two days of daycare a week, so I decided I would have breakfast, lunch, and happy hour meetings those days. I was doing five networking events minimum per week—two to three lunches and two to three evening events. Looking back now, I think that's insane, but that's what I did."

The results weren't immediate, but they were lasting. "I've had people hire me ten years after they heard me speak," she shared. "They say, 'I heard you; you made an impression, and I kept your card. I didn't need it at the time, but now I really need you.'"

Instead of traditional advertising, Sona focused on being present where her ideal clients might be. "I thought about where my ideal clients would hang out? Who would they talk to? I would rent kids' indoor playgrounds and have parents come while their kids were being watched, and I'd talk about estate planning. But I also targeted financial planners, family law attorneys, CPAs—people who are in touch with my clients."

One of her most successful referral sources came from an unexpected place—entertainment industry professionals. "Entertainment clients are actually very good networkers because that's how they get their jobs," she explains. "I just got a new client from Dreamworks who told me, 'We have an internal Slack channel, and your name always comes up as the person to call.'"

The Power of Strategic Relationships

"These days, my networking looks very different," Sona explains. "Those seeds I planted years ago are still bearing fruit. I'm much more intentional with my time now because I don't have as much time for evening events and weekend meetings. But all those relationships I built? They've deepened into real connections."

Her approach to maintaining these relationships is refreshingly straightforward: "I don't just refer people I've just met off the street. When I refer someone to my clients, it's someone who's been vetted, and whose work I've seen personally. I even hire my own clients; my client Jeff is renovating our backyard right now. If clients trust me with their stuff, I will trust them."

This two-way street of trust has created a powerful referral network. But Sona emphasizes it's not about tracking favors: "I give without expecting anything back. If you're counting how many referrals you've given versus received, you're missing the point. People call me for recommendations about everything because they know I'm connected. That makes me look good, and the referrals naturally follow."

She's become known as a connector in her community. "When I look at my group of friends, I'm often the singular person who brought all these people together. I do that in my neighborhood a lot; I see somebody walking with a little kid, and I think, *Oh, you should meet my friend Danny.* Danny says I've introduced her to the whole neighborhood without her having to do anything."

The results speak for themselves. "At Halloween, three different clients came trick-or-treating at my house. I didn't even know they lived nearby. They recognized me and said, 'Sona, you did our estate plan!' That's the kind of community connection you can't build with billboards."

But perhaps most importantly, Sona has built exactly the kind of practice she wants. "I'm in 100% control. If I want to bring on two associates and get more business, I could do that. But right now, this is what I want—working from home, making dinner for my family every night. Everyone thinks having a large firm is the goal, but that's not necessarily the case. You need to know what makes you happy and what's going to make you feel fulfilled."

From Hustle to Harmony

"Being intentional is everything," Sona emphasized as we wrapped up our conversation. "I get invited to hundreds of events, but I think carefully about where I can be of most help to others and what fits best with who I am and what I practice." She shared a crucial insight that changed her approach early in her career: "We often try so hard to get better at things we're not good at, instead of focusing on things we're good at and actually trying to improve those. I was in court every day, fighting with people, and it was eating at me. That's not what I'm good at. I'm good at building relationships and working as someone's advisor."

This philosophy extends to how she runs her practice. "I'm very protective of my time now. When I do lunch meetings, I only do them close to my house. I won't drive across town to Century City anymore. I work from home, and I value my time with my family more than chasing every networking opportunity."

But perhaps her most valuable advice comes from her experience starting out: "When I first started the practice, I put everything I earned back into the firm. I hired help immediately. My husband thought I was crazy, but I knew I needed to give things I'm not good at to somebody else. Because what's most important is bringing in clients, serving them well, and letting others handle the rest."

Sona's approach proves that marketing doesn't have to mean advertising budgets and billboards. It can be as simple—and as challenging—as being intentionally excellent at building relationships and knowing exactly who you want to serve.

Let's break down what makes Sona's marketing approach so effective and how you can apply it, regardless of your practice area.

First, consider how Sona solved a common marketing challenge: trust. Estate planning involves discussions about death, money, and family—topics that make most people uncomfortable. Instead of trying to overcome this resistance through traditional marketing, she positioned herself as someone who understands these concerns firsthand. As a young parent herself, she could relate to her target clients' fears and hesitations. This authenticity became her strongest marketing tool.

Her approach created what marketers call "network effects." By focusing on young families in entertainment and professional circles—groups that naturally share information—each successful client interaction multiplied her reach. That Dreamworks Slack channel didn't appear by accident. It grew because she consistently delivered value to a well-connected community.

You can apply this same principle to your practice.

A business attorney might become deeply involved in

local entrepreneur groups, chambers of commerce, and startup incubators. Real estate attorneys can build relationships with property developers, mortgage brokers, and real estate agents who work with their ideal clients.

Family law practitioners often find success networking with therapists, financial advisors, and divorce coaches. Criminal defense attorneys can develop relationships with bail bondsmen, substance abuse counselors, and social workers who often encounter people needing legal representation.

Immigration lawyers naturally connect with cultural organizations and international business groups, while employment lawyers might focus on HR professional associations and accountants providing payroll services. Personal injury attorneys can build relationships with medical professionals, chiropractors, and physical therapists.

Intellectual property lawyers might find their ideal clients through technology meetups and inventor associations. Tax attorneys can network with CPAs, financial planners, and business brokers. Entertainment lawyers often find success connecting with talent agencies, production companies, and business managers.

The key isn't just joining these groups, it's becoming a valuable resource within them. Offer to speak at their events, contribute to their newsletters, or serve on their boards. When you position yourself as a helpful expert rather than just another lawyer looking for business, the referrals flow naturally.

Sona's "give first" mentality also offers a masterclass in professional networking. Rather than tracking referrals like an accountant's ledger, she focused on being genuinely helpful. This approach turns traditional networking on its head. Instead of trying to meet potential clients, she concentrated on building relationships with other professionals who could help her clients.

But perhaps her most valuable lesson is about sustainable marketing. Those early years of intense networking built a foundation that still generates clients today. She didn't just collect business cards, she built real relationships that deepened over time. Now she can be more selective with her time while maintaining a steady flow of ideal clients.

The message is clear: Effective marketing isn't about having the biggest advertising budget or the most aggressive social media strategy. It's about being intentionally excellent at what you do, deeply understanding who you serve, and building genuine relationships within your chosen community.

Your marketing strategy should feel as natural as having a conversation with a friend. Because ultimately, that's exactly what it is.

KEY TAKEAWAYS:

- **Build Your Brand Through Relationships:** Marketing doesn't require a big advertising budget. It requires intentional relationship building and a clear understanding of who you want to serve.

- **Network With Purpose:** Focus your networking efforts where your ideal clients gather or where their trusted advisors operate. Quality connections beat quantity every time.

- **Give Without Keeping Score:** The most successful referral networks grow from genuine helpfulness, not transactional relationships. Focus on being a valuable resource rather than tracking favors.

- **Start Strong, Then Scale Back:** Invest heavily in relationship-building early in your practice. These foundations will continue generating clients even when you reduce your networking time.

- **Stay True to Your Vision:** Build the practice you want to run, not the one others think you should have. Success comes in many forms; define yours intentionally.

Conclusion

Throughout this book, we've explored the critical elements that transform a law practice from a demanding job into a thriving business. From proper trust accounting to strategic marketing, from building systems to creating sustainable growth, each chapter has provided specific strategies to help you take control of your practice's future.

Let's take a moment to reflect on the key principles we've covered:

We started by examining why so many lawyers find themselves trapped in the hamster wheel of daily practice. Remember Ms. IP from Chapter One? Like many attorneys, she was excellent at practicing law but struggled with the business side of running a firm. She was making good money but working around the clock, missing her children's events, and feeling more like an employee than a business owner. Her story illustrates a crucial truth: Technical legal expertise alone isn't enough to build a sustainable practice.

This realization led us to explore the importance of systems and processes. As we saw with Mark, David, and Sarah's story, implementing proper systems isn't just about efficiency, it's about creating a practice that can thrive without requiring your constant attention. When they finally stepped back and invested time in documenting procedures and training the team, their billable hours actually increased while their stress levels decreased.

We dove deep into the financial aspects of running a successful practice. The numbers don't lie, and as we discussed, you can't improve what you don't measure. Think about it this way: How would you know how much weight you need to lose if you never step on a scale? You might have a general sense that your clothes are tight, but without specific numbers, you're just guessing. Running a law practice is no different. How can you know where you're going if you don't know exactly where you are?

Proper bookkeeping isn't just about satisfying regulatory requirements, it's about having the data you need to make informed decisions about your firm's future. Those who track their KPIs and understand their numbers are the ones who can make strategic decisions rather than reactive ones. Just like that scale gives you the feedback you need to adjust your diet and exercise, your financial metrics tell you exactly what's working in your practice and what needs to change.

Remember Sona's marketing strategy? Her success wasn't built on expensive advertising campaigns but on intentional relationship-building and a deep understanding of her ideal clients. By focusing on young families and becoming deeply embedded in her community, she created a referral network that continues to generate business with minimal ongoing effort.

The trust accounting chapter served as a sobering reminder of what's at stake. The Tom Girardi case showed us how even the most successful practices can implode without proper financial controls. But more importantly, we learned that maintaining impeccable trust accounting isn't just about avoiding trouble. It's about building a foundation of trust that allows your practice to grow.

We explored the power of niching down and becoming known for something specific. Like the attorney who focuses exclusively on Hispanic businesses or Sona's concentration on young families, the most successful practices aren't trying to be everything to everyone. They've found their sweet spot and own it completely.

Throughout all of these discussions, one theme has remained constant: the importance of focusing on what you do best and delegating the rest. You went to law school to practice law, not to become an accountant, bookkeeper, or business manager. Yet these functions are critical to your success.

This understanding of law firm operations didn't come from textbooks or theory. It came from years of working exclusively with attorneys, seeing their challenges firsthand, and developing solutions that actually work in the real world. I've walked alongside hundreds of lawyers as they've built their practices, sharing their struggles and celebrating their successes.

The patterns become clear when you focus on a single industry. Most law firms face similar challenges, from trust accounting compliance to strategic growth decisions. But more importantly, every firm has unique opportunities that only become visible when you have the right financial insights and systems in place.

Having a financial partner who understands the specific demands of running a law practice changes everything. When your accounting team speaks the same language—understanding the difference between contingency fees and retainers, knowing the intricacies of trust accounting, recognizing the patterns in law firm cash flow—you can focus on practicing law rather than explaining basic concepts.

This kind of specialized support isn't just about keeping books or preparing tax returns. It's about having someone in your corner who can help you spot opportunities, avoid pitfalls, and make data-driven decisions about your firm's future. It's about transforming financial management from a source of stress into a strategic advantage.

The goal isn't just to maintain compliance or track numbers. It's to give you the freedom to focus on what you do best while knowing the business side of your practice is in capable hands.

The road ahead is clear. The legal industry is becoming more competitive, more regulated, and more complex every day. The firms that will thrive are those that build strong foundations, implement proper systems, and focus their energy where it matters most—serving their clients and growing their practice.

You've already taken the first step by reading this book

and understanding what's possible. The next step is implementation. However you decide to chart your course, remember that success in legal practice isn't just about being a good lawyer. It's about building a business that serves your goals and supports your vision.

The path forward is clear. You can keep trying to be a lawyer, accountant, HR manager, and marketing director all rolled into one, though I wouldn't recommend it unless you've figured out how to clone yourself or stop time. Or you can acknowledge that even Superman had a team behind him (and presumably a good accountant to handle his freelance journalist taxes).

Every successful law firm started somewhere. Many started exactly where you are now, trying to juggle too many balls while secretly wondering if anyone else finds it this challenging. Spoiler alert: they do. The difference between those who continue struggling and those who break through often comes down to a simple realization: Asking for help isn't a sign of weakness, it's a strategy for success.

The most successful attorneys we work with didn't get there by being great at everything. They got there by being great at what matters most—practicing law and building relationships with their clients. They found the right partners to handle the rest. After all, you wouldn't advise a client to handle their own complex legal matter just because they've watched every episode of *Suits* would you?

Think of it this way: Your expertise as a lawyer didn't come from trying to figure it all out on your own. You went to law school, learned from experienced professors, maybe worked at a big law firm for a few years, and probably had mentors along the way. Building a successful practice isn't any different. The smart play is learning from those who've been there before.

At the end of the day, your legacy won't just be measured by the cases you've won or the clients you've served. It'll be measured by the practice you've built, the lives you've impacted, and yes, by the number of your kids' soccer games you actually made it to.

Building a successful practice isn't about working yourself to the bone or sacrificing everything for the sake of growth. It's about creating something sustainable, something that works for you instead of demanding every waking moment of your life. It's about having the time to be both a great lawyer and a present parent, partner, or whatever else matters in your life.

Remember that personal injury attorney we discussed earlier, the one who thought meticulous settlement tracking was enough for trust accounting compliance? Last I heard, he's sleeping through the night again now that he has proper systems in place. Turns out having someone else handle your three-way reconciliations isn't just good business, it's good for your mental health too.

The practice you've always wanted is possible. One where you're doing the work you love, making the impact you envision, and maybe even making it home for dinner more than once a quarter. Now wouldn't that be something?

Sources

(Thomas Girardi section)

- Los Angeles Times extensive coverage of the Girardi case
- Federal court documents from Girardi's criminal case
- Netflix documentary coverage
- California State Bar investigation reports
- Court documents from Ruigomez case
- Federal sentencing documents from 2023
- Various legal news sources including Law.com and ABA Journal
- NTSB Report on Lion Air Flight 610
- Federal Court Criminal Indictment USA v. Girardi
- Los Angeles Times investigative series on Girardi
- California State Bar Investigation Reports
- Boeing settlement documentation
- Court transcripts from Girardi's sentencing
- FBI investigation documents
- Civil litigation filings from multiple victim cases
- Indonesian Aviation Authority crash report
- California Bar Journal disciplinary records
- Federal Bankruptcy Court proceedings
- Various victim impact statements from sentencing

Acknowledgments

To my parents, who made the boldest decision of their lives—leaving everything behind with three young children to move to a country they had never visited, all to give us opportunities we could never have had in Iran. Dad worked 12 to 14 hours a day, seven days a week, to secure our future, while Mom somehow managed to work and raise us. They taught us life's most important lessons not through words, but through their unwavering example.

To my brother and sister, who constantly challenged me as their youngest sibling and gave me a childhood I couldn't have experienced without them. Even today, they remain a support system that only those with close siblings can truly understand.

To my wonderful sons, William and Henry, who have given my life new meaning and motivation to work smarter every day so I can be present in ways my father couldn't be with me. They wake me with their smiles, and I put them to bed with a smile on my face—life's perfect bookends.

And finally, to my amazing wife, who trusted me from day one—even when I was laid off just one month before our wedding. She never doubted me for a moment, and continues to support me every day without question. The saying "behind every successful man stands a strong woman" resonates deeply with me because I've lived its truth.

About the Author

Emil Abedian's journey from immigrant to renowned financial expert uniquely positions him to guide law firms toward unprecedented success. Born in Iran to Armenian parents during a time of political upheaval, Emil was just four years old when his family fled to Sweden following the Iranian Revolution. Growing up in a new country, he developed the resilience and adaptability that would later become hallmarks of his business approach.

Despite the challenges of immigrant life, Emil thrived in Sweden, eventually graduating from university and beginning his career at Ernst & Young in Stockholm. His path took an unexpected turn when a visit to Los Angeles introduced him to his future wife, prompting him to relocate to the United States in 2007.

Today, as Founder and CEO of Counsel CPAs, Emil has established himself as the premier financial strategist for law firms. His firm exclusively serves attorneys, providing specialized accounting, tax planning, and strategic advisory services that transform law practices into thriving businesses. Drawing from his experience in both global accounting firms and boutique practices, Emil has developed a comprehensive approach to law firm management that consistently delivers exceptional results.

Emil's unique perspective—shaped by his multicultural background and immigrant experience—allows him to see opportunities where others see obstacles. His clients value not only his technical expertise but also his approachable style and genuine commitment to their success. When not revolutionizing law firm operations, Emil enjoys spending time with his wife and two sons, occasionally reminiscing about the freedom of his Swedish childhood while creating new traditions in America.

Through this book, Emil shares the strategies and insights that have helped countless attorneys escape the hamster wheel of overwork and underearning to build sustainable, profitable practices that serve both their clients and themselves.

For more information or to contact the author,
visit **www.counselcpas.com**